MW01121306

2007 12 03

DATE DUE	RETURNED
NOV 1 6 2009	NOV 2 5 2009

THE ODYSSEY

A PLAY ADAPTED FROM HOMER

The Odyssey

A play adapted from Homer

by
Rick Chafe

Playwrights Canada Press
Toronto • Canada

Playwrights Canada Press
54 Wolseley Street, 2nd Floor
Toronto, Ontario CANADA M5T 1A5
(416) 703-0201 fax (416) 703-0059
info@puc.ca http://www.puc.ca

Playwrights Canada Press acknowledges the support of The Canada Council for the Arts for our publishing programme and the Ontario Arts Council.

ONTARIO ARTS COUNCIL
CONSEIL DES ARTS DE L'ONTARIO

Cover by Doowah Design Inc.
Cover photo of Megan McArton and Nelson Tomé by Paul Martens Photographer Inc.
Production Editor: Jodi Armstrong

National Library of Canada Cataloguing in Publication Data

Chafe, Rick
 The odyssey: a play adapted from Homer

ISBN 0-88754-613-7

I. Homer. Odyssey. II. Title.

PS8555.H265O39 2001   C812'.54   C2001-901911-4
PR9199.3.C466O39 2001

First edition: July 2001
Printed and bound by Hignell Printing at Winnipeg, Manitoba, Canada.

For Martine and Charlotte.

ACKNOWLEDGEMENTS

While most of the dialogue in this adaptation is original, many lines and phrases are taken from Homer, modified from the four translations I relied on: Samuel Butler, E.V. Rieu, Robert Fagles, and Robert Fitzgerald.

The play's development was greatly assisted by two workshops, and the present form of the script owes a tremendous debt to the contributions of the workshop actors, Debbie Patterson, Arne MacPherson, Raye Anderson, Wayne Nicklas, Czilla Przibislawsky, Lora Schroeder, and Jason Neufeld, as well as to the cast of the first production. Chris Gerrard-Pinker provided structural ideas, theatrical guidance, and inspiration throughout the writing.

Thanks also to Margaret Sweatman, Yvette Nolan, Kim McCaw, Ulla Ryum, Carl Ridd, Per Brask, Shakespeare in the Ruins, Moe Hicks, St. Norbert Arts Centre, Louise May, Katie East, Laura Farn, Lauro Genzale, Brenda Belmonte, Sue Stone, Shane Stewart, The Manitoba Association of Playwrights, Rory Runnels, Angela Rebeiro, Playwrights Canada Press, and most especially to Martine Friesen.

Financial assistance to support the writing and workshopping of this play was generously provided by the Manitoba Arts Council.

PLAYWRIGHT'S NOTES

The stage directions are intended to be evocative rather than literal. The first production took place outdoors, in and around the ruins and grounds of a former Benedictine church and monastery – Hermes rode a scooter and Circe's home was a tree house; a very effective cyclops was created variously by multiple off-stage voices, then by shadows, and finally by an actor standing over paper cut-out sheep; the ship took many forms for the different scenes, all of them created with the actors' bodies. With a few minor line re-assignments to accommodate multiple roles, all the parts were covered by nine actors.

In mythology, Helen and Clytemnestra were half-sisters by the same mother; Penelope was not related to them by blood. I have made all three half-sisters to strengthen their roles as foils to one another, which is implicit in Homer.

The Odyssey was first produced by Shakespeare in the Ruins at the St. Norbert Arts Centre in Winnipeg, September 13, 2000, with the following cast:

•PENELOPE	Megan McArton
•THE STRANGER	Wayne Nicklas
•YOUNGER ODYSSEUS, EURYMACHUS	Arne MacPherson
•EURYCLEIA, ATHENA, GIARDINO, POLYPHEMUS, GHOSTS, SIREN	Sarah Constible
•TELEMACHUS, ASTEUS, SID, AGAMEMNON, GHOSTS	Eric Blais
•CALYPSO, MELANTHO, JONESY, GHOSTS, SIREN	Daina Leitold
•HERMES, AMPHINOMOUS, NAUSICAA, GEORGE, GHOSTS, SIREN	Michelle Boulet
•CIRCE, ANTINOUS/ BOLETUS, SOLO, ANTICLEIA, TIRESIAS, GHOSTS, SIREN	Debbie Patterson
•EURYLOCHUS, DORION, IRUS, ACHILLES, GHOSTS	Tom Soares

Directed and dramaturged by Chris Gerrard-Pinker
Set Design by Leanne Foley
Costume Design by Catherine Green
Lighting Design by Scott Henderson
Music by the Cast
Stage Manager – Marlene Meaden
Assistant Stage Manager – Amanda Smart

CHARACTERS

ATHENA (a-THEE-na) goddess, daughter of Zeus, patron of ingenuity, resourcefulness, wisdom

YOUNGER ODYSSEUS (o-DIS-yoos) the king of Ithaca, looks at least 20 years younger than the Stranger

CALYPSO (ka-LIP-soh) a nature goddess/nymph

AMPHINOMOUS (am-FI-no-mus) a suitor to Penelope

BOLETUS (bo-LEE-tus) suitor

ASTEUS (a-STEE-us) suitor

DORION (DOR-ee-on) suitor

ANTINOUS (an-TI-no-us) suitor

MELANTHO (me-LAN-thoh) a palace maid, friendly with the suitors

EURYMACHUS (yoo-RI-ma-kus) leader of the suitors

PENELOPE (pe-NE-lo-pee) the queen of Ithaca, same age or younger than the Stranger, at least 20 years older than her suitors

EURYCLEIA (yoo-ri-KLEYE-a) Penelope's ancient handmaid, old enough to have been nurse to Odysseus

THE STRANGER at least 20 years older than Younger Odysseus, same age or older than Penelope

IRUS (EYE-rus) the palace beggar

NAUSICAA (naw-SI-kay-a) a young princess of Phaeacia

EURYLOCHUS (yoo-RI-lo-kus) first mate to Odysseus

SOLO crew to Odysseus

SID crew

GIARDINO (jee-ar-DEE-no) crew

JONESY crew

GEORGE crew

LOTOS EATERS

POLYPHEMUS (po-li-FEE-mus) the cyclops

CYCLOPS NEIGHBOURS at least two voices

AEOLUS (EE-oh-lus) god of the winds

TELEMACHUS (te-LEM-a-kus) son of Odysseus and Penelope, 20 years old

HERMES (HUR-meez) messenger of the gods

CIRCE (SIR-see) a goddess/witch

ANTICLEIA (an-ti-KLEYE-a) mother of Odysseus, now a ghost in Hades

ACHILLES (a-KIL-eez) famed Greek warrior at Troy, now in Hades

AGAMEMNON (a-ga-MEM-non) supreme commander of the Greeks at Troy, now in Hades

TIRESIAS (teye-REE-si-as) blind seer of Thebes who retains powers of prophesy in Hades

GHOSTS helpless spirits of the dead in Hades

SIRENS enchantresses of the sea

1. ATHENA AND CALYPSO

Darkness. ATHENA enters with a sweet song.

ATHENA

Sing in me, muse, of the man
Man of tricks and twists and turns
Master of war, long castaway
Sing the tale again

Father Zeus, Athena calls
Your daughter's heart breaks for my friend
Plagued with wandering years on end
Sing the tale again

Ten years at Troy he pleased you well
Ten years more kept on the seas
Twenty years from home, release him now
Sing the tale again

If it please the blissful gods,
The exile must now return
Let Odysseus see his home
Sing the tale again

ATHENA watches as a tranquil island takes form in early evening light, and she then leaves. The YOUNGER ODYSSEUS stares out over an endless ocean. A nature goddess approaches – the nymph, CALYPSO. She watches him; his eyes stay on the ocean.

CALYPSO

How so, unlucky one?

YOUNGER
ODYSSEUS

Evening so soon?

CALYPSO

Is all this so hateful? This island—my alder and pungent cypress, my meadows, violets and parsley, the springs clear and bubbling, the red grapes growing by my cave—has none of it ever pleased you?

YOUNGER ODYSSEUS	Even a bird dies sooner in a cage.
CALYPSO	Odysseus. This cup is ambrosia. The gods drink from it, never to lose their youthful looks, never to die. The cup is immortality.

He ignores the cup; she drops it.

Once you came to me freely. Now I steal every night with magic charms. Mornings find my sheets unwound and you pouring tears into the sea. My heart isn't iron. I have tools. Build your raft.

YOUNGER ODYSSEUS	Calypso – after seven years you'd let me go?
CALYPSO	I'll give you food and water. Warm clothes and a following breeze.
YOUNGER ODYSSEUS	Cross the ocean on a raft? Great ships aren't safe. No raft of yours, not unless you swear my safety.
CALYPSO	My oath?

The mortal I saved from Poseidon's ocean, half dead, all his shipmates killed by Zeus himself. This mortal man I've cherished. Loved, fed, sang to that you should never grow old. This mortal I could never harm.

(*beat*) With the earth then, as my witness, the sky and the black waters of Styx, by the most solemn oath sworn by the gods, I have no more magic, no more intrigues to work against Odysseus. All I devise for you and all that I tell are just as if your wants and mine were one.

YOUNGER ODYSSEUS	Calypso...

CALYPSO
It isn't my oath you need.

The gods bed mortal women with as much thought as passing wind, and yet they are scandalized when a goddess lies beside a mortal man. And now they turn their jealous eyes on me for keeping my mortal companion. The gods who tormented you would now send you home.

YOUNGER ODYSSEUS
The gods send me? The journey's on.

CALYPSO
With such pains ahead, you'd never leave this island if you knew.

YOUNGER ODYSSEUS
What disaster have I not endured already? Bring your tools, I'll build the raft.

CALYPSO
Straight back to Poseidon's ocean? All this for her?

YOUNGER ODYSSEUS
Aye. Bring on the trial.

CALYPSO
This Penelope you weep for every day... how can she rival a goddess? In beauty? In grace? Can she be more subtle? More desireable?

YOUNGER ODYSSEUS
Great Calypso. My Penelope is an ordinary woman. She could seem only a pale shadow beside you – how well I know that. And yet all I long for is to see her again.

CALYPSO
Twenty mortal years Odysseus. I've held back the years for you. Who stops time for your ordinary woman? No matter what graces the gods heap upon you, you can't believe you'll find your home as you left it.

YOUNGER ODYSSEUS
Yet find it I must.

CALYPSO   Then tell Zeus to swear you a sweet journey
                 home. Tell him you'd have a gentle reunion
                 with your ordinary woman. I don't think
                 you'll get it.

                 *CALYPSO leaves him. ODYSSEUS prepares
                 his raft. He is oblivious to ATHENA, as he
                 lifts a sail and launches out against thunder
                 and a furious sea, clinging to his mast.*

ATHENA   Crafty, ingenious, lying pirate. Mastermind
                 who contrived the fraud of the great
                 wooden horse. Sacker of cities who burned
                 great Troy to the ground. Wiley snake who
                 survived ten years pursued by the great
                 Poseidon himself. We are of the same
                 weave, Athena and Odysseus, both lovers
                 of tricks and deceit – that's why I have never
                 deserted you in all your cruel fortune.

                 One last adventure, Odysseus, and then we
                 part. Master of war, can you master your
                 own home?

                 *ATHENA, ODYSSEUS and the sail
                 disappear with the sea.*

2. THE SUITORS

                 *Ithaca. Evening in the palace courtyard.
                 The suitors have a luxurious rough camp
                 beneath PENELOPE's window, touches of
                 elegance within filth. Beautiful jewellery,
                 fire barrels, discarded mutton bones, farting.
                 ASTEUS and DORION gamble.
                 AMPHINOMOUS, very drunk,
                 ANTINOUS and BOLETUS share a bottle.
                 Throughout the scene, MELANTHO—a
                 palace serving maid—comes and goes; she is
                 intimately familiar with any number of
                 the suitors.*

AMPHINOMOUS   *(toasting)* Ahhh home, home, home. God,
                 I don't want to go home.

BOLETUS	Stay, baby, stay, stay, stay.
AMPHINOMOUS	Money, sweetheart, money money.
ASTEUS	Daddy won't pay his bills no more.
DORION	No no, daddy won't pay his bills no more.
AMPHINOMOUS	*(calling up to the window)* Penelope! Come out, darling, say goodbye!
VOICE	*(from off)* More wine!
AMPHINOMOUS	Enough of this! We should put a sword to her throat right now. "Penelope? Who do you love the best. It's me, right?" I knew it! She loves me! She loves me!
DORION	She loves him!
ASTEUS	Oh Sweetness!
BOLETUS	Take my sword, Prince, go find your love.
ANTINOUS	Beat her a few with the broadside first, let her know you're serious.
VOICE	*(from off)* More wine, I said! Bring some more bloody wine!
AMPHINOMOUS	*(calling up to her window)* Penelope! Three years now! Come say goodbye!
EURYMACHUS	*(entering)* Ha! I've got it!
VOICE	*(from off)* Who do I have to kill to get some service? I want wine, I want it now!
EURYMACHUS	*(calling up to the window).* Penelope!
AMPHINOMOUS	Go ahead. Bust a lung.
EURYMACHUS	*(calling up)* Penelope, it's Eurymachus.

ASTEUS Give her my love if you ever see her.

EURYMACHUS *(to the others)* There are a hundred and seven princes in this courtyard now. I think we can make better use of all this royalty.

DORION What better use?

EURYMACHUS For starters, the queen is about to choose a husband.

ASTEUS I'd see your money on that one, Prince.

EURYMACHUS *(throwing his purse on the ground)* Match it, Prince, you'll lose.

(calling up) Three years, Penelope. If the gods woo slowly, what's time to them? But mortals must be prudent gardeners. Court in springtime, marry in summer. No earthly gardener waits to plant in December.

ASTEUS Very nice, bring up age to a woman.

ASTEUS drops a purse to match the first one; BOLETUS drops another purse beside it.

EURYMACHUS *(to the suitors)* I was in the harbour just now. I counted fifty ships. Fifty! And every prince with one ship in Ithaca has at least ten more at home. We could get up to something useful here, lads.

(calling up) Three years, Penelope. Surely we've made an impression by now?

DORION What are you jabbering about, Eurymachus?

EURYMACHUS *(to the suitors)* The queen's son is missing. Telemachus is twenty years old now. If he were to return, would you have him take his rightful place on his father's throne? And one of us marries a queen without a kingdom? Think on that.

(calling up) When do you stop dreaming of a dead husband Penelope? Beautiful youth when he left, they say. But twenty years? What would Odysseus look like today if he still lived, I wonder? Imagine the scars a soldier must carry, cut after cut, year after year, tearing away at his good looks, his good manners, his pleasant, cheerful disposition. Plenty of beauty down here, Penelope. Stout hearts, strong legs, name the features, they're in your courtyard.

(to the suitors) What a wonderful springtime of youth we've had here, lads. Time to grow up. I propose we turn our minds to the common business of our kingdoms.

DORION   What "business?"

EURYMACHUS   Piracy.

DORION   *(sputtering with laughter)* "Piracy??"

BOLETUS   You'd have us risk our own lives?

ASTEUS   Actually get in sturdy black ships like our dear old fathers and hunt for wealth?

EURYMACHUS   Modern piracy, Prince. Not one kingdom sacking another. One hundred kingdoms sacking all others. One by one by one.

BOLETUS   After three years just give up on Ithaca?

EURYMACHUS   We settle Ithaca right now. One prince takes this lovely Queen and her kingdom to be treasured. One hundred princes take the whole world. It's time to end the queen's game. Penelope will choose a husband now.

DORION   And why do you think you can suddenly force this queen to do anything?

EURYMACHUS   Because you and I are intelligent men. And
                    because I know where Prince Telemachus is.

                    (calling up) I have news I think you'd want
                    to hear, Penelope. Concerning your family,
                    news from the outside world...

                    PENELOPE opens her window, veiled.

PENELOPE   Enough caterwauling Eurymachus, you're
                    worse than all these drunkards put together.

EURYMACHUS   I'll howl until I see the face I came for, Lady.
                    At least step into the light.

PENELOPE   The light left with my son. Speak your news.

EURYMACHUS   And if your son doesn't return? Just add
                    him to the total? How many young men will
                    you spend your life waiting for?

PENELOPE   You've learned cruelty in your time here.

EURYMACHUS   I've learned plain speaking. I can end this
                    stalemate and bring peace back to your
                    palace.

PENELOPE   Peace is a luxury, your offer is rejected. Get
                    to your news.

EURYMACHUS   With one hundred princes in the courtyard,
                    I think her majesty has overplayed her hand
                    too long. These drunkards may think it's
                    time they called the game.

PENELOPE   Are you openly threatening me?

EURYMACHUS   I'm conducting business.

                    (turning to the suitors) One hundred princes,
                    I offer my services as marriage broker. This
                    is the single largest wedding contest since
                    our dear fathers flocked to the famous Helen
                    – our own queen's beautiful sister.

But our good fathers didn't dally with courtships forever. They drew together and swore an oath: to honour and protect the marriage of Helen's choice. And what an alliance came of that oath! When our queen's beautiful sister forgot her marriage vows, our valiant fathers tore the invincible city of Troy to the ground and dragged her back!

Isn't Helen's sister worthy of such an honour?

All swear an oath now, in name and witness of Penelope, this company is united to uphold the honour of her marriage—as she chooses—to one of our company!

> *To great laughter and cheers, one by one, the suitors raise their hands and call "Sworn!" until all are done.*

Your suitors, my Queen. Choose wisely and you'll marry the most powerful man in the greatest alliance ever to rule these oceans.

PENELOPE   You count honour by numbers and treat courtship as war. I'll give you neither.

> *PENELOPE turns from the window.*

EURYMACHUS   *(calling after her)* I also promised news of your family.

> *Beat. She returns.*

Prince Telemachus is in Sparta, visiting King Menalaus, your husband's old friend. He's very well and was to leave for Ithaca today. If his travels are uneventful he should be home in three days at the latest. But as I know your concern I will personally send a ship out to escort him safely home.

ANTINOUS   I will accompany that ship with one of my
                  own.

DORION   And I'll send another.

BOLETUS   And another.

AMPHINOMOUS   And ten more of mine.

PENELOPE   Eurymachus, understand this. When my son
                  left a month ago I gave him up for dead.
                  I won't resurrect him now for you to
                  ransom. Your presence in my house was
                  merely distasteful, it is now impossible.

                  She exits. Pause.

EURYMACHUS   I'll provide Cyprean wine while we await
                  her decision.

                  The suitors laugh and cheer.

                  And Gentlemen – learn to recognize that
                  queen's bluffs or you'll never master her
                  bed.

                  We will sail to the strait and intercept
                  Telemachus, yes?

ANTINOUS   My ship is ready.

DORION   I'll have three ships for you guarding
                  the harbour. Much as I detest sailing, my
                  soldiers don't.

EURYMACHUS   Well done, Princes. Our future bodes well.

                  All exit.

3. THE BALANCE

PENELOPE frantically paces her chamber. EURYCLEIA, an ancient handmaid, stands by.

PENELOPE

"Give up. Give up. Are you mad? Do you want to die this way? Give up!" Twenty years. Holding this island, keeping home and family, my youth dried up, the vultures circle. I cannot stand it any longer, Eurycleia, I will break.

I wait, and my son grows up without a father. I wait, and Ithaca demands a new king. I wait, and the suitors eat their way through my fortune. I wait, and my son disappears in the night. I wait... and this pack of drunken imbeciles suddenly grow up into assassins.

It ends. My husband is dead. Only Telemachus now. Only my son.

EURYCLEIA

Then choose one and marry. If you don't, they will kill Telemachus, that's the only certainty.

PENELOPE

Is that certain? Will they spare him if I marry, or murder him to end the line? No choice is good, the wrong move kills him. Only the gods know his fate and they tell me nothing.

EURYCLEIA

Nothing nothing nothing. It's your son's life, and you do nothing.

PENELOPE

I showed hope, and gave them the weapon against me. I dare not breathe, Eurycleia. At this moment my son is equally alive and dead, I hang on the balance. This face, this body, will not betray me again. This body wears a second skin, this face a mask.

Watch at the window. Any sign the balance tips, I will move like a scorpion.

EURYCLEIA moves to the window; PENELOPE retreats to the shadows. Laughter erupts from below.

4. THE STRANGER

The Courtyard. A loud yell from the STRANGER as he's thrown in through a doorway among the suitors, followed by IRUS — the palace beggar — and the suitors' laughter.

STRANGER   Attack an old man from behind? What kind of vermin are you?

As the STRANGER tries to stand, IRUS kicks him down, the suitors hoot.

IRUS   My door, old rotbag. You want to beg, find your own door.

STRANGER   Call it off, or I'll break that nose of yours.

IRUS   Ho! You want to try me old man?

More hooting from the suitors.

BOLETUS   One gold coin on Irus!

ASTEUS   One gold coin on the stranger! Get in there champ!

DORION   Two gold coins on Irus!

EURYMACHUS   Two gold coins on the stranger!

The STRANGER and IRUS circle to the suitors' goading.

*Above in PENELOPE's chamber. The sounds
of the fight continue, as EURYCLEIA looks
out the window.*

EURYCLEIA   It's an old man, being bullied by the princes.
He must be the beggar that showed up with
the pigs this morning.

PENELOPE   A beggar? From where?

EURYCLEIA   Away. Dropped off by a boat last night.
Told the swineherd unbelievable stories for
hours, had him completely charmed – says
he's been everywhere, knows the whole
world.

PENELOPE   *(going to the window)* Let me see.

*Back in the courtyard, the STRANGER is
beaten by IRUS. Suitors cheer and boo
according to their bets and exchange coins.
EURYCLEIA calls from the window.*

EURYCLEIA   Melantho!

MELANTHO exits into the palace.

EURYMACHUS   *(beckoning)* Grandfather!

*The STRANGER, panting and hurt, turns to
him.*

You cost me two gold coins.

STRANGER   I'm not as young as I once was.

EURYMACHUS   I'll call it a debt. You can work it off.

STRANGER   Your highness is a prince among thieves.

EURYMACHUS   Old man, are you looking for a fight with
me now?

MELANTHO   *(calling out from the doorway)* The Queen
                  would see the old man in her chambers.
                  Immediately.

AMPHINOMOUS   You're joking.

STRANGER   I'm no company for a lady. Please tell her
                  no.

ANTINOUS   You festering old blister.

BOLETUS   Are you defying the queen?

STRANGER   I'm better suited to this rough crowd.

EURYMACHUS   My beggar. Tell me. Have you ever slept
                  with a queen?

STRANGER   *(beat)* Forgive me. I'm unused to Ithacan
                  humour.

ANTINOUS   What – rough talk offends the beggar?

ASTEUS   Come listen at our table tonight.

DORION   Half the men here will share stories of their
                  sport with this queen.

EURYMACHUS   We only mention it so that you keep an eye
                  open for an advantage. Who knows, you
                  may be just her type.

                  Suitors laugh.

                  (kicking him) Go you stinking old tramp!
                  Keep your appointment with her majesty!

                  *The suitors push the STRANGER towards
                  the palace.*

5. THE BEGGAR AND THE QUEEN

PENELOPE's Chamber. EURYCLEIA is
present with PENELOPE. The STRANGER
stands, head bowed.

PENELOPE   My suitors downstairs – you've had time to
watch them?

STRANGER   A few minutes.

PENELOPE   They threaten my son. He's missing. His
name is Telemachus. Have you seen him?
Heard anything, anywhere in your travels?

STRANGER   No. Nothing.

PENELOPE   You've been overland, near Sparta? The
southern coast? Any of the nearby islands?

STRANGER   I've heard nothing. Surely he could still be
safe?

PENELOPE   Safe on the seas? My husband disappeared
on the seas ten years ago.

Every month since brings more suitors to
Ithaca. They run my servants ragged, eat me
out of house and home, determined to force
a marriage upon me.

What can I do? Zeus's laws demand
hospitality for guests. I have no soldiers,
the council won't stand up to the suitors,
Ithaca wants a new king. Every day brings
false rumours, false signs of my husband's
return. This morning, flocks of birds, fraught
with meaning, declare his arrival. How can
I any longer trust birds?

The suitors hunt my son now, I'm sure of it.
If I marry, I may save his life... or hasten his
death. Tell me, Beggar. What would you
have me do?

STRANGER	You ask me this?
PENELOPE	Beggar... I ask.
STRANGER	*(beat)* If your marriage is sacred.... If you still love your husband.... If you've remained true all these years... then surely your heart holds your answer.

Long pause.

PENELOPE	Wise beggar. You have your leave and my thanks. Eurycleia. We prepare for a wedding. Call them to the window, I'll speak to them.

EURYCLEIA opens the window.
PENELOPE goes to it.

STRANGER	Madame... *(beat)* I know something of your husband.
PENELOPE	*(beat)* My dead husband?
STRANGER	His whole story these last ten years.
PENELOPE	Skip to the end.
STRANGER	It's uncertain. It's three months and a great distance since I heard it from his lips.
PENELOPE	He lives.
STRANGER	Safe on the seas?
PENELOPE	Maybe alive, maybe dead? Assassins chase my son – what are you offering me?
STRANGER	I've repeated the whole of his story to myself, every day for three months. I offer you every word as Odysseus spoke them.
PENELOPE	My son's life against my husband's words?

STRANGER   Believe me, I seek hope as dearly as you do...

PENELOPE   You can't possibly.

EURYCLEIA   *(beyond containment)* Madame...

PENELOPE   No counsel Eurycleia. *(beat)* There are one hundred and seven dogs in that courtyard who would tear you to pieces to win my favour. Tell it. Zeus save you if I detect a lie.

STRANGER   Where I met him then.

I was a castaway, survivor of a shipwreck, afloat for days. Some river goddess had pity on me, pulled me in to her cove, the shore of an island, battered, half-dead. Until I woke to the sound of young voices.

6. PHAEACIA

A child's ball comes rolling around a corner into the room. Three young girls run out after it, but seeing the STRANGER and PENE-LOPE, two of them run back. The last, NAUSICAA, stands staring at the STRANGER.

STRANGER   Princess – Are you goddess or mortal? Please show mercy. I've suffered endless torment, show me the way to town, a rag to cover my nakedness, and may the gods grant all your heart desires.

NAUSICAA   Stranger, I'd say you're not an evil man and no fool. If Zeus hands you suffering you must bear it. But having reached our city, you'll never lack for gifts. Our city is Phaeacia [Fee-AY-sha], my father is king here and can grant you all you wish. Come.

> NAUSICAA leads the STRANGER and
> PENELOPE around the corner; we leave
> Kansas and suddenly we're in Oz, where we
> find...

7. ODYSSEUS

> A dinner table in the Phaeacian palace....
> NAUSICAA's young friends welcome the
> STRANGER and PENELOPE as dinner
> guests. The STRANGER takes a seat as
> PENELOPE stands apart, watching.

STRANGER Homeless, a poor beggar, treated like royalty at a lavish table, where I ate and listened to wondrous music and entertainments. Until a bard sung an ode of Troy, the battles fought there, the famous men who had fallen, and of the great wooden horse, built by the master of craft, Odysseus, that spelled the end of hope for the city of Troy.... And hearing it all, another stranger, another wanderer washed up on those shores, at the same dinner table, another man weeping at the song. The dinner guest turned to our hostess, and said,

> At a distance, PENELOPE sees a man stand
> up. It's the YOUNGER ODYSSEUS,
> speaking at the same time as the
> STRANGER, more quietly than the
> STRANGER at first, but then growing to
> match his volume, as the image and memory
> of him becomes stronger.

**STRANGER &
YOUNGER
ODYSSEUS** "My Queen, I am Odysseus, son of Laertes, known to all mankind for every manner of guile. My fame has reached the heavens, but my sorrow has never been told..."

> *Her eyes fixed on the YOUNGER*
> *ODYSSEUS, PENELOPE comes to the*
> *dinner table; the STRANGER guides her by*
> *the hand to a chair as he spins the story.*

YOUNGER
ODYSSEUS   *(speaking alone, full voice)* My home is the
island of Ithaca, under Mount Nion
[NEYE-on], wrapped in a wind-swept robe
of green. The sun shines always, the land is
rugged, a good country for raising sons.

STRANGER   *(speaking alone)* "You ask me the cause of my
sorrow," he said. "In telling it I'll have cause
for more. Where can a man find sweetness
greater than his own home? Not in distant
travels, though he seeks the ends of the
earth and gains a house of gold.

"Where, then, have I been since Troy?" he
said.

STRANGER &
YOUNGER
ODYSSEUS   What of those ten stormy years weathered
under Zeus?

8. TROY

> *Torches light fire barrels as Troy burns. The*
> *dinner guests jump up — suddenly they are*
> *Ithacan soldiers of the Greek army, pillaging*
> *Troy's riches and fighting off Trojan soldiers.*
> *EURYLOCHUS — the second in command —*
> *is dumping everything of value into a sack;*
> *SOLO and SID sample the wine and food as*
> *they steal the dinnerware.*

EURYLOCHUS   Cups, plates, candlesticks! All of it, grab and
go, grab and go!

SOLO   That's nice. That's a sweet cup.

SID	This cup's worth more than all I've owned in my whole sorry life.
GIARDINO	*(enters coughing)* Blasted smoke – I think my lungs are collapsing. They send us in and start torching the place already, my knees are killing me – these stairs–
SID	Greeks have no idea how to make wine.
SOLO	We're primitives compared to Trojans. I'll miss them.
JONESY	*(entering with a prize)* Hey – look at this knife! You ever see anything so beautiful?
EURYLOCHUS	Forget the knives, we want gold!
JONESY	Are you kidding? Look at it, feel the balance–
EURYLOCHUS	Come on, that's only one sackful, get moving before the roof comes down.

> *YOUNGER ODYSSEUS meets them at the doorway.*

YOUNGER ODYSSEUS	Ahh! Good Ithacan lads. *(beckoning)* Look. The horse is burning.

> *They peer out a window at the great horse, burning in the city square.*

EURYLOCHUS	Goodbye, Mother Nelly. You carried us well.
YOUNGER ODYSSEUS	Was that a trick? Was that a piece of carpentry?
SOLO	General, that was a long night to spend curled up beside this foul-smelling brute *(meaning SID).*

**YOUNGER
ODYSSEUS**   No more "General", the war's over. Head
back to Ithaca if you can't wait to see home,
but I know an island—just three day's
sailing out of our way—with a town rich
enough to load down every ship and just a
tiny band of shepherds to protect it. I've got
eleven boatloads of Greeks signed on, but
for real adventure, a captain wants Ithacans
at his side.

EURYLOCHUS   We're in, Captain – every one of us. Right?

SOLO   What do you wanna do, Sid?

SID   I dunno, what do you wanna do, Solo?

SID & SOLO   Yeah! We're in!

**YOUNGER
ODYSSEUS**   Giardino?

GIARDINO   My back is broken three different ways,
someone rows for me, I sit beside the
biggest, meanest, strongest rower or I don't
step on board.

**YOUNGER
ODYSSEUS**   Ah, my hearts, my boys! The world is out
there, let's go find it!

*The crew cheers and begin preparing their
ship.*

STRANGER   Thousands sailed back to their homes – the
men he loved best came with him. Twelve
ships – three hundred men. Alinous – the fat
soldier who killed three Trojans by sitting on
them. Darius – the best spearman in any
army, Greek or Trojan...

**YOUNGER
ODYSSEUS**   Zorba – carpenter and cook, we'll eat well.
Antilious – luck is the only thing kept him

alive this long. Lefty—plagued by gas—try not to get a seat next to him, it's a long ride. Harold, George, and Stanley – inseparable, saved each other's lives a dozen times. Dear Michael; poor Michael. Yahooti, wonderful musician, Desmond, the idiot.... The little house painter who made such a great archer; the stone mason who I promoted to corporal; that incredibly brave plumber who lost his arm to a Trojan sword...

STRANGER ...Nathanial, no legs and ears, lopped off by Trojan steel, and Jonesy who arrived with eleven toes and left with all of them! This crew, these men–

PENELOPE Stranger—my husband—what did he look like?

STRANGER *(beat)* A young man he seemed – face and body younger than his years. Skin still supple, lithe limbs, russet curls.

One thing stands out. A golden broach to clasp his cloak. I'll never forget it. On the face a hound clenching a fawn in its forepaws, the fawn slashing as she writhes. A marvellous piece – at one moment it seems the dog is sure of victory, but you look again and no, the fawn is about to master him.

PENELOPE *(pause)* Twenty years and you bring my wedding gift back to me. Thank you for that, Stranger.

Your story.

STRANGER *(beat)* Precious men, he had. A hundred more whose names he never learned. He loved them, he took care of them, lives are more precious than we could ever know.

9. THE GOLDEN ISLAND

> *By now all the crew are rowing, most prominent is GIARDINO, rowing beside little GEORGE.*

YOUNGER ODYSSEUS   Well I don't know but I heard it's true–

ALL CREW   I don't know but I heard it's true–

YOUNGER ODYSSEUS   Trojans make good barbeque.

ALL CREW   Trojans make good barbeque.

YOUNGER ODYSSEUS   Sound off–

ALL CREW   One, two–

YOUNGER ODYSSEUS   Sound off–

ALL CREW   Three, four– One, two, three, four, three, four– One Two!

GIARDINO   My arms will buckle – pull George. Three days, let me off, I'll walk home.

YOUNGER ODYSSEUS   That island! Down the hillside, below the meadows. See the town? Look close.

SID   It sparkles – every house...

SOLO   They trim their windows with gold?

EURYLOCHUS   They never heard of pirates?

> *The crew cheers, piles off the boat and disappears over the hillside.*

**YOUNGER
ODYSSEUS** George! Stand lookout – fair share for everyone! One hour, lads—quick strike and we're back in the boats—take only what you can carry, we're out before they know what hit them, one hour–

GEORGE climbs to a lookout point above ODYSSEUS. EURYLOCHUS returns, with an armful of gold door knobs.

EURYLOCHUS Door knobs! The ninnies use golden door knobs!

EURYLOCHUS dumps the door knobs and runs back.

**YOUNGER
ODYSSEUS** Eurylochus! Just what you can carry – that's enough!

EURYLOCHUS *(calling back)* There's a whole village full of these!

GIARDINO *(dumping golden window shutters at GEORGE's feet)* I think I tore my back in two – half of it's yours, George, load it will you, friend–

**YOUNGER
ODYSSEUS** Giardino – no more time–

GIARDINO *(calling back)* I'm just going back for the front door!

**YOUNGER
ODYSSEUS** George, what time?

GEORGE Going on two hours at least.

**YOUNGER
ODYSSEUS** Call them in.

GEORGE Call!

         A trumpet blast.

YOUNGER ODYSSEUS What's keeping them?

GEORGE They're loading up wagons!

YOUNGER ODYSSEUS We can't carry all that! Call again!

GEORGE Call!

         Another trumpet blast.

None coming!

YOUNGER ODYSSEUS What's all the noise that way?

GEORGE *(climbing higher)* Horses!

SID *(returning over the hill)* Hundreds of them!

SOLO *(returning)* They're fully armed!

YOUNGER ODYSSEUS Load! Load! All in!

         Trumpets blast over and over. ODYSSEUS helps men pile into the boat as GEORGE watches until the last moment.

Load! Load! George! Any more? Anyone?

GEORGE None! I can't see! None!

YOUNGER ODYSSEUS All in! Pull out! Pull out!

EURYLOCHUS *(coming over the hill)* One more!

         EURYLOCHUS dives for the ship.

CREW MEMBER Pull! Pull! Get out of here, move!

**YOUNGER
ODYSSEUS**   Gone! Move it George!

                *GEORGE jumps aboard. GIARDINO isn't
                on the bench beside him. GEORGE begins to
                row with the others.*

ALL CREW   *(loudly)* Pull! Pull! Pull! Pull!

                (softer) Pull! Pull! Pull! Pull!

STRANGER   Far outnumbered, a third of them were
                slaughtered, six benches left empty in every
                ship.

10. THE LOTOS EATERS

                Slow rowing.

ALL CREW   Damn sea. Goddamn sea.

                Damn sea. Goddamn sea.

EURYLOCHUS Pack together. Dump the spare oars.

                Slow rowing continues.

JONESY   I kept my knife.

SOLO   I met a girl.

SID   You have enough time?

SOLO   Didn't touch her. Reminded me of my wife
                when I met her.

EURYLOCHUS Getting homesick?

SOLO   If my wife was still fifteen. She's thirty-five
                or something now. Six kids. When I left
                anyway. Not homesick for any of that.

**YOUNGER
ODYSSEUS**   *(surveying the crew)* Giardino?

GEORGE   Didn't make it. Or Darius.

JONESY   I saw Julian go down and Antilous.

EURYLOCHUS   Yahooti, Alinous, Desmond...

STRANGER   They sailed onward with sorrow in their hearts. But Zeus raised the North wind against them till it blew a hurricane. Night sprang forth from the heavens, bows plunging, sails cracked, winds tearing them to rags. They saw death in that fury... two nights and two days they laid up, cringing from the storm.

The crew crouches, covering heads, holding onto each other, a tangled rocking mass.

The third day, shining dawn came spreading fingertips of rose. A gentle wind blew them on...

A beautiful, lazy, wordless song comes floating from away.

...to the land of the Lotos Eaters. People of perfect contentment, who eat the leaves of the lotos all day long. And never want for anything.

YOUNGER ODYSSEUS   *(calling orders)* Solo, Sid, Jonesy, investigate and report.

The three leave, ODYSSEUS settles in to wait.

SOLO, SID & JONESY   ...Damn rain. Goddamn goddamn rain...

Still covering their heads, the crew members come across the singers of the tune, a group of locals, sprawled in the rain, some clearly enjoying it, others oblivious to it.

*As naturally as a cat stretching, the locals —
gently singing the whole time — offer lotos
to the crew, who taste it. They're quickly
overcome with sensations. They feel the rain
and enjoy it. Some take off excess clothing.
They caress each other, mark their faces with
mud. JONESY begins brushing himself with
a lotos leaf and makes a discovery.*

JONESY   Tongue!

*The others brush their bodies with the leaves,
discovering they can taste with their arms,
stomachs. They begin touching the ground,
the grass, tasting everything around them
with their bodies... then the air... JONESY
makes another discovery.*

Atoms!

*After a moment of staring extremely closely
at objects, SID giggles.*

SID   Trojans...

They all laugh.

SOLO   Family...

They laugh.

JONESY   Philosophy.

They laugh.

SID   Love.

*They laugh, then go silent, becoming
perfectly still, exploring something absolutely
invisible. EURYLOCHUS, ODYSSEUS and
other crew come looking for them.*

EURYLOCHUS   What in hell's name have they been
drinking?

YOUNGER **ODYSSEUS**	*(shaking the men)* Sid. Solo.

ODYSSEUS tugs at SOLO. He resists.

Jonesy – come on, old whore. It's raining.

JONESY Leave me.... It's... paradise.

SID reaches for more lotos, ODYSSEUS takes it from him.

YOUNGER
ODYSSEUS *(kindly to the three crewmates)* I lost a hundred men in one hour. I won't lose one more man on this voyage.

He waves and suddenly the other crewmates are on them, dragging them crying, back to the ship.

SID *(whining)* Lotos...

YOUNGER
ODYSSEUS Back to the ship! All hands aboard! No one eat the lotos or lose all hope of ever seeing your home!

SID, SOLO, and JONESY, back on the ship, go fetal, and then slowly move together, huddled for comfort, while the crew rows, PENELOPE and the STRANGER still following from nearby.

11. POLYPHEMUS

STRANGER Some god must have guided them that night, they could barely see the mast in the dense fog. They glided into shallows so gently, they didn't know they'd made land until gracious dawn pushed back the mist.

EURYLOCHUS revives, suddenly realizing he isn't rowing anymore.

EURYLOCHUS   Out... out... OUT! Get me off this damned boat, I wanna eat, I wanna kill something!

EURYLOCHUS runs over a hill. Other crewmates wander out from below and into the light, JONESY, SID and SOLO still mildly shaking from lotos withdrawal.

CREW   Sun.... Sun.... Sun...

EURYLOCHUS   *(returning for the rest)* Rabbits and gulls' eggs, ten feet away! Breakfast!

ALL CREW   *(moaning with appetite)* Breakfast... breakfast... breakfast...

YOUNGER ODYSSEUS   *(pointing)* Smoke rising from a fire! Just twelve I'll need, the rest enjoy your day on the beach. Time to see whether our neighbours are wild savages or good, hospitable, god-fearing men.

EURYLOCHUS climbs the mast as look-out.

EURYLOCHUS   Sheep! Lots of them! In corrals made of stone. Huge slabs of it. And one bastardly big cave... with one bastardly big rock beside it...

STRANGER   The land of cyclops. Giants, lawless brutes. In ignorance they neither plow nor plant, though grain and grapes grow on that rich land without tending. Cyclops have no law, no social ways, no custom, each living to his own, caring nothing for his brothers.

YOUNGER ODYSSEUS packs two wineskins.

YOUNGER ODYSSEUS   Come on. We'll take gifts – maybe we'll get something better in return.

JONESY

Captain, the size of his house, he'll drink more than two bags of wine.

YOUNGER
ODYSSEUS

This is a real gift – Trojan brandy. One cup mixed with twenty cups of water is still stronger than you or I could stand.

EURYLOCHUS

Captain, he uses that huge rock for a front door.

YOUNGER
ODYSSEUS

Who knows what kind of gifts we'll get from a man that size? If he's heard of Zeus, he'll respect strangers.

EURYLOCHUS

And what if he's so big and ignorant he hasn't heard of Zeus?

YOUNGER
ODYSSEUS

Eurylochus, we have to know, don't we? What kind of life would you have if you'd stayed home in Ithaca all these years?

PENELOPE

(calling out) You'd know your son.

YOUNGER
ODYSSEUS

(beat, then answering as if Eurylochus had asked) But would you have a story worth telling him?

> *Beat. ODYSSEUS and the crew enter the dark cave.*

EURYLOCHUS

(disgusted) Well, he stinks.

> *JONESY chews a fistful of the giant's cheese.*

JONESY

He makes good cheese!

> *SID finds a wine keg and drinks, then spits.*

SID

His wine's like horse piss!

SOLO

Captain, let's take the cheese, take his sheep, get out of here before he comes home.

**YOUNGER
ODYSSEUS**

Why travel the seas and keep your eyes
clamped tight? Just for gold? Eat the cheese,
laugh with your friends.

> *Suddenly the sound of a great walking step, a
> huge drum, louder and louder. All the men
> scramble into a single hiding space.*

Eurylochus, what do you see?

> *EURYLOCHUS peeks out as the drum
> reaches its loudest.*

EURYLOCHUS

He's a great hairy mountain. His walking
stick's as tall as the ship's mast. One eye
only? He only has one, great, huge eye!

> *The footsteps stop. EURYLOCHUS ducks
> back into hiding. A huge voice surrounds
> them.*

POLYPHEMUS

What are thee? Pirates?

> *ODYSSEUS steps forward.*

**YOUNGER
ODYSSEUS**

We are Greeks on our way home from Troy,
but by the will of Zeus we have been driven
far out of our course. We humbly pray you
to show us hospitality, and such gifts as
custom would have you give visitors. May
you take care, great sir, to respect your duty
to the gods, for Zeus is the avenger of all
unoffending guests.

POLYPHEMUS

We Cyclops think nothing of your blessed
gods – we are stronger than them. But tell
me. I'd like to see your ship. Is it close by?

**YOUNGER
ODYSSEUS**

My ship? Poseidon broke it on the rocks at
the far end of your land, these men and I the
only survivors.

The other crew members timidly peek out.

POLYPHEMUS   Ha.

*Two of the men scream as they're dragged
away.*

STRANGER   The monster grabbed two men, one in each
hand like wriggling puppies, and smashed
their brains out, spattering the floor. He
pulled them to pieces and made his meal,
tearing and crunching as we watched, crying
and lifting our hands to Zeus. Then he rolled
the huge boulder against the door, and
stretched out like a felled tree among his
sheep.

*ODYSSEUS draws his sword, signals to the
crew.*

**YOUNGER
ODYSSEUS**   Ten swords left, straight through the liver.

They creep close, draw their swords to strike.

JONESY   Once he's dead... who's gonna move that big
rock?

*Pause. The whole crew absorbs the trap
they're in, lower their swords in despair.*

STRANGER   A long night without sleep. The monster
rolls over...

*A great rolling rumble – the crew all hold
their breath.*

...and goes back to sleep. They wrack their
brains for a plan.

In the morning, he eats two more men for
breakfast...

Screams from the crew.

...rolls the boulder from the door...

Remaining crew watches in hope.

...goes out... and rolls it back.

Their hope dissolves.

But Odysseus had his answer.

SID   He'll never leave the door unblocked.

EURYLOCHUS   If we don't kill him tonight there won't be enough of us left to do it.

JONESY   And then we die slowly.

SOLO   At least he goes too.

YOUNGER ODYSSEUS   He left his walking stick. Sharpen it. Scrape it smooth. We need a spear.

The crew takes up a large pole.

Work it, carve it, sharpen it, harden it in the fire. Keep your courage up. One chance is all we need. And when he comes home...

Footsteps; everyone runs for cover.
ODYSSEUS steps forward.

Good host! Your name, sir?

POLYPHEMUS   For all the good it will do thee to know, Polyphemus.

YOUNGER ODYSSEUS   Polyphemus, I brought you this good wine hoping to win your friendship. Now I see what kind of barbarian you are, I can only hope to win your pity.

ODYSSEUS pours wine for the monster.
Huge gulping sounds.

POLYPHEMUS	More. Don't be cheap with it.
YOUNGER ODYSSEUS	You like my wine, Polyphemus?
	More glugs.
POLYPHEMUS	The gods thou lovest so would call this ambrosia. Now tell me thy name so I can offer a gift to warm thy heart.
YOUNGER ODYSSEUS	Nobody.
POLYPHEMUS	Nobody? That's a name?
YOUNGER ODYSSEUS	My name is Nobody. My father gave it to me and I've had to carry it all my life. What guest gift do you have for me, Great Polyphemus?
POLYPHEMUS	Nobody – Thy friends come first, I'll eat thee last. There's a noble guest gift to thee. Ha. Good night.
	POLYPHEMUS falls asleep.
YOUNGER ODYSSEUS	Now – the spear, heat it in the fire, harden it till it glows red, and all to places. More than natural force we need now, pray Zeus to fill arms and legs and drive hard.
	Together they take up the spear, and ram it into the eye of the cyclops. An explosion of noise and terror.
STRANGER	From outside the cave, the monster's neighbours answered his screams.
SECOND CYCLOPS	*(from outside the cave)* What ails thee, Polyphemus?

THIRD CYCLOPS	Thou wakes my family with wailing!
SECOND CYCLOPS	Who attacks thee? Who hurts thee?
POLYPHEMUS	Nobody!
SECOND CYCLOPS	Nobody?
POLYPHEMUS	Nobody is attacking me! Nobody is killing me!
THIRD CYCLOPS	Then what good can we do thee? Your troubles must come from the gods!
SECOND CYCLOPS	Pray to thy great father, let it be he that helps thee.
POLYPHEMUS	Nobody! Thou will suffer for this far worse than what thou has caused me! Where are thee?

POLYPHEMUS crashes about in search.

POLYPHEMUS	The door is open, Nobody. Try to walk past me.
STRANGER	How to win the game, with death guarding the door? How to get out? How to slip away?
POLYPHEMUS	Will thou trick me with sleep again? I can go twenty nights without sleeping, how long can thou last?
STRANGER	Odysseus cudgeled his brain, conjured plan after plan, scheme after scheme, until the trick came, and it pleased him well.

We hear the bleating of sheep.

POLYPHEMUS   My sheep will see the sunshine. I never
               again will, will thou? Did thou come
               planning to steal the giant's treasures? How
               would a pirate like thee know what I call
               treasures?

STRANGER   The giant felt for his sheep as they passed
               beneath him, but Odysseus tied the rams
               together in threes, with one man tied
               beneath the middle of each three. Guarded
               from the giant groping fingers, the men
               passed to freedom. But none were left to
               prepare the Captain's passage.

                    The sheep pass beneath the cyclops.

               The largest, the woolliest of the rams,
               Odysseus took for himself. He hung from
               the fleecy belly, dug fingers deep into the
               ringlets.... But this one animal, the giant
               stopped at the door.

POLYPHEMUS   Sweet old ram, thou never lingers – always
               first to the freshest grass, first to the stream,
               first to turn home for the night. Why so far
               behind this morning?

               Sick at heart for thy master's eye, can that be
               it? Nobody will not get out alive, I swear. If
               thou had voice to tell where he hides, this
               hand would bash his skull till his brains
               flew all over the cave. And I'd ease my heart
               of the suffering I owe him.

STRANGER   And speaking thus, he drove the ram
               outside.

                    *The crew run for the ship, pack in and begin
                    to row.*

               They ran his whole flock down to their
               ships, back to their friends, faces shining to
               see them, then turning to grief in counting
               the numbers missing. But far out to sea, as

far as his voice would carry, Odysseus sent words back to the monster.

YOUNGER ODYSSEUS Polyphemus! A weakling am I, to a giant like you?

EURYLOCHUS Godssake, Captain!

SID What are you doing!

YOUNGER ODYSSEUS Eat up guests in your own house? Zeus and the gods have paid you for it!

POLYPHEMUS yells and hurls a huge rock, splashing ahead of the boat, just missing the crew, and driving the boat back to shore.

(shouting) Polyphemus–

SOLO Shut up, you idiot!

YOUNGER ODYSSEUS –if anyone asks who spoiled your beauty–

EURYLOCHUS Don't give him a target for the next one!

YOUNGER ODYSSEUS –say it was Odysseus, raider of cities, say it was he who took your eye, the son of Laertes, Odysseus of Ithaca!

POLYPHEMUS *(crying out in anguish)* A wizard foretold my great eye would be lost to Odysseus. Always I watched for some armed giant to defeat me honourably, by strength. But an ordinary little man – in trickery–

(turning to the heavens) Poseidon! Hear me, great Poseidon; if I am indeed thy son and thou my father, grant me this: that Odysseus of Ithaca, son of Laertes, may never reach his home. If Destiny must take him there, make

that day far and fill the years between with misery. Let him return alone, a broken man, and find in his home a world of pain.

STRANGER   Then Polyphemus picked up a rock much larger than the first, swung it over his head and sent it flying.

It fell just short of the rudder, and the sea quaked from the wash of the wave it raised, driving the ships onwards, away from his island. Escaped with their lives, but not their friends.

Long pause, the STRANGER watches PENELOPE.

My queen? I've touched on something.

PENELOPE   It's nothing.

STRANGER   It's not.

PENELOPE   Ten years gone, now you tell me he's under Poseidon's curse? No great surprise, fishermen's wives know the power of the sea.

STRANGER   A fisherman's wife sheds tears.

PENELOPE   You want tears? Improve your chances, tell your story to that wall.

STRANGER   On the water then. Windless days. Too long to row dawn to dusk, even in shifts.

12. THE ISLAND OF THE WINDS

The crew sits in their benches, exhausted. SID stares at the water.

SID   Cursed. I've been cursed... two hundred times in my life? I never believed it before.

EURYLOCHUS	You really believe he's Poseidon's son? You'd take a monster's word on that?

SOLO is fingering a medallion at his neck.

JONESY	Hey. That's a nice piece.
SOLO	Got it from that girl. Sitting in her golden house.
JONESY	What girl?
SOLO	She thought I was going to rape her.
EURYLOCHUS	You seriously saying you didn't think about it?
SOLO	I was thinking about being fifteen again.
EURYLOCHUS	You just talked.
JONESY	For a whole hour?
SOLO	I couldn't leave. And the longer I stayed the more scared she got. So I told her just... just sit. I said, talk, just talk to me, just anything.
SID	*(spotting something in the distance)* Smoke rising...
EURYLOCHUS	Land...
STRANGER	The island of the winds. You never find it in the same place twice, it floats, blown about at the whim of its master, Aeolus [EE-oh-lus], god of the winds.
	Aeolus has six sons and daughters – he marries them one to another, then divorces them... and re-marries in new combinations. All to provide amusement and endless celebration. He greeted the men like kings, and entertained them a full month.

Crew members meet daughters and there is much merriment. Small moments of dance and love might spring up.

And when it was time to part, Aeolus gave the captain a great parting gift...

AEOLUS Only one wind will blow for the next nine days—a stiff westerly—taking you straight home. And this–

AEOLUS presents ODYSSEUS with a huge bag.

Keep it closed until you're safely on your home shore.

YOUNGER ODYSSEUS *(overwhelmed)* Farewell...

There are great sad and tender farewells, but also a great swelling joy.

And now – home!

SOLO Wind!

SID Wind!

JONESY Wind!

SOLO Merciful Zeus! This is what they mean by sailing.

SID Nine days to home!

JONESY I still got my knife.

SID Eight days to home!

SOLO Take a rest Captain, I'll take the tiller.

ODYSSEUS waves him off.

JONESY Five days to home!

SID	What the hell, maybe I'll get married.
GEORGE	Three days to home!
SOLO	I still kinda don't miss my wife...
SID	Two days to home!
JONESY	Captain, give it a rest, you can't stay awake forever!
ALL CREW	One more day!
EURYLOCHUS	What do you suppose is in that bag?
SID	Gold probably.
EURYLOCHUS	Of course it's goddamn gold. Captain gets the best gifts everywhere he goes and we just get to row.
JONESY	It's the lighthouse! We'll be there in an hour!
EURYLOCHUS	Am I the only one that thinks we get a share of that?
GEORGE	There it is!
SID	Houses!
SOLO	Home!
JONESY	Home!
GEORGE	Home!
EURYLOCHUS	We just take it, right, Solo?
	ODYSSEUS is yawning.
SOLO	I'm in.
EURYLOCHUS	I'm opening it, you want some, Sid?
SID	I'm in – open it.

SOLO   Go – just go, he's asleep...

                   ODYSSEUS is sound asleep on the tiller. The
                   crew members rip the bag open and freeze,
                   suddenly aware of what's in the big empty
                   bag. The winds tear from every direction.

STRANGER   And every wind, every gust, every
                   hurricane, from every direction that had
                   all been safely bagged up came roaring out
                   of the sack and blew the ships... all the way
                   back to the floating island of Aeolus. Where
                   the king—now knowing the Captain must
                   be hated by the gods, the most cursed man
                   alive—sent him on his way, no helpful
                   breeze in sight.

PENELOPE   *(beat)* Beggar.... Fathom a dream for me.

                   I keep twenty geese behind the house. One
                   of my few delights is to watch them pick
                   at grain by their pond. In my dream I'm
                   feeding the geese, stroking them. But down
                   from the sky swoops a great mountain eagle,
                   and he snaps their necks—every one—
                   and leaves their broken bodies in heaps
                   throughout the halls. Back he soars into the
                   blue skies, and I wail. The eagle killed my
                   geese. But down he drops again and calls
                   out: "Courage, queen! The geese were your
                   suitors, and I am your own husband, home
                   again to bring a terrible revenge on every
                   man among them."

STRANGER   There's no mystery, it means what it says,
                   Odysseus told you himself – he'll return and
                   he'll make death for every suitor. It's a clear
                   and strong sign from the gods themselves.
                   Your waiting will be rewarded.

PENELOPE   But dreams unravel hard, even the simplest
                   – some arrive through gates of truth, but
                   some are false top to bottom. Which do we
                   trust?

STRANGER	What does your heart tell you? What would you do?
PENELOPE	Answer, honestly this time.
STRANGER	How?
PENELOPE	These geese, I loved them.
STRANGER	And so...?
PENELOPE	The eagle said they were my suitors. I wept for them.
STRANGER	You thought they were geese when you wept...
PENELOPE	No other thought occurs to you?
STRANGER	Not one I'd dare think. Do you tell me you have love for these suitors?
PENELOPE	It's nothing. Go on.
STRANGER	*(beat)* More islands. Storms. Horrible creatures, nightmares. Of twelve ships that started out, one remains.

13. PIGS

Aboard ship. JONESY is looking up at the stars. EURYLOCHUS approaches.

EURYLOCHUS	Beautiful island. Going ashore?
JONESY	See that?
EURYLOCHUS	*(looking up)* What?
JONESY	The Little Bear usually looks straight down at the Big Bear.
EURYLOCHUS	It's looking the other way...

JONESY

The planets are supposed to follow the Zodiac. For a week they've been wandering all over the sky. Back home this time of night the Milky Way spreads North to South. It's spilling West to East. The stars are lost.

All I can say is, I'm glad it's the Captain's boat we're on.

YOUNGER ODYSSEUS

(entering) Good news! A twelve-point stag in one arrow – sent by a god to cheer us. Venison for supper!

EURYLOCHUS

I thought for sure he was going to say he's found some giant's castle.

YOUNGER ODYSSEUS

And on the far side of the island – a column of smoke.

Shoulders drop, men bury their faces in their hands.

Come friends. We've seen terrors, but we can't pass up a chance for help. Twelve straws—six long, six short—short straws leave after eating.

All pull straws, ODYSSEUS pulls long.

EURYLOCHUS

(pulling short) Well, look at that. If I only had the Captain's luck.

YOUNGER ODYSSEUS

Eurylochus. You would still be in Troy, alive or dead, if I hadn't built the horse. You would still be in the Cyclops' cave, passed through his gut, if I hadn't got you out.

EURYLOCHUS

(under his breath) I would never have left home if you hadn't dragged me. No man alive would enter a giant's cave without a madman for a Captain.

YOUNGER ODYSSEUS   Eurylochus, lead your group. We'll stay by the ships until your return.

The group goes off, leaving ODYSSEUS and JONESY.

My son is twelve years old now.

JONESY   Mine too.

YOUNGER ODYSSEUS   We'll be home for their thirteenth birthdays.

STRANGER   The story becomes more painful.

PENELOPE   I'll hear it.

EURYLOCHUS returns running, barely able to speak for breath and terror.

EURYLOCHUS   Up the woods – a palace in a glen, a marble house – sweet song, someone sitting at her loom – they all said, "nothing to fear, just a young girl with a pretty voice." She opened the door – a beautiful woman, a temptress, a sorceress, I'm sure of it.

STRANGER   Closer, perhaps, to the heart.

PENELOPE   I will hear it.

EURYLOCHUS   I stayed back, I smelled deceit. "Come in" she called – they went, and didn't come out, I kept watch for hours, all gone, no sign...

PENELOPE   *(to the STRANGER, cooly)* Fix your eyes elsewhere. You're the entertainment, not me.

YOUNGER ODYSSEUS   Come back with me, take me the way you came.

EURYLOCHUS   Even you, Captain, I know it, even you
won't come back–

**YOUNGER
ODYSSEUS**   Eurylochus–

EURYLOCHUS   Take the men that are left, let's get in the
boats, save ourselves while we can.

**YOUNGER
ODYSSEUS**   *(contemptuously)* Take shelter. Be safe with
the boats. My duty is to seek out this
temptress.

14. TELEMACHUS

     *As YOUNGER ODYSSEUS goes off,
EURYCLEIA enters.*

EURYCLEIA   Madame...

     *PENELOPE wheels, eyes flashing at the
interruption.*

PENELOPE   *What.*

EURYCLEIA   Privately?

PENELOPE   *(to the STRANGER)* You trouble me. You're
not as you appear.

STRANGER   I'm old... I've been many things...

PENELOPE   You reek of nobility.

STRANGER   They say my father was not the man who
raised me. It may be true.

PENELOPE   You watch my eyes too closely for a beggar.

STRANGER   Then I've become the most laughable fool,
the beggar in love with the queen.

> *Beat. PENELOPE turns to EURYCLEIA; the STRANGER turns away.*

EURYCLEIA Telemachus. He's outside the door.

> *PENELOPE gasps, but holds it in.*

PENELOPE *(referring to the STRANGER)* Keep him in sight. He's a born spy, his eyes ferret the soul. Use your wits, plumb him, find out anything you can, don't leave him in a room without bolting the door.

Stranger. My hospitality offends you. My servant will bathe you and offer fresh clothes.

STRANGER I decline your great kindness.

PENELOPE And I insist. That door.

> *EURYCLEIA leads the STRANGER through an alternate exit. The main door opens.*

PENELOPE Telemachus...

TELEMACHUS *(entering)* Mother...

> *(She grips him.)*

I'm sorry—

PENELOPE You're alive. Did anyone see you?

TELEMACHUS I came through the woods.

PENELOPE Everything is all right now. Everything, sweet light of my eyes. Can you have grown in a month? I swear you've taken on years. We'll get you away. You'll go to your father's cousins, we still have many friends. If I could I'd lock you in a box, you'll break my heart again.

TELEMACHUS	Ithaca is my home, Mother, I'm staying here.
PENELOPE	The princes won't let you live. Once you're safe I'll marry and they won't think of you again. And that's an end of it at last.
TELEMACHUS	This is my home and my inheritance. I will not leave it.
PENELOPE	I'll keep you hidden until tomorrow night, because I can't bear to lose you again sooner. Even that's foolish.
TELEMACHUS	It is foolish. This house belongs to me and I will have it.
PENELOPE	Listen to me–
TELEMACHUS	You listen now. You will marry, yes, and I will choose your husband. It's my right, I'm twenty years old, I'm no child anymore. I've spoken with a goddess–
PENELOPE	*(stony)* What goddess.
TELEMACHUS	Athena herself. Who walked with my father. You have no idea, Mother. I know the world of ships, and men, grown warriors. I've talked with kings and sons of kings. I've heard all the stories of Troy, from the men who fought there. I've heard all of my father's battles, from the men who fought beside him. I know how the horse was built, the cherry wood, the wedged wheels, the twelve men who sat in its belly sweating through the night. I've met Menalaus, the great general–
PENELOPE	Menalaus is an idiot.
TELEMACHUS	Ha! I know – he married your sister, not you, didn't he? Two hundred men all courted Helen. I know all about it, I met her, I've seen her myself, she's incredible, she's

still beautiful and she's almost as old as you!
And I know she's the daughter of Zeus. I'm
sorry, Mother, but I know this is true, isn't
it? Three sisters, three fathers – your mother
would lie down with anyone, like Helen ran
off across the sea with a prince–

PENELOPE This is what you learned from your
goddess?

TELEMACHUS This is what I learned from Helen herself,
from Menalaus, from Nestor—the oldest and
wisest general at Troy—all my father's
friends. I learned about Clytemnestra, your
other sister – you know what I learned,
don't you – the wife of the great
Agamemnon – she took a lover while
he was at Troy, when he came home the
two of them caught Agamemnon in a net
and killed him with a club. I saw her
picture, I see the resemblance–

PENELOPE Do you? Do you see anything?

TELEMACHUS I have seen, every day, for three years, my
mother acting the whore, like her mother,
like her sisters, talking favours to a hundred
men, in my house–

PENELOPE Your father's house–

TELEMACHUS My father is dead!

PENELOPE I will say when he's dead!

TELEMACHUS *(grabbing her)* If he's not dead, you're not free
to marry!

*His touch releases a hammer spring in her –
she belts him hard and fast.*

PENELOPE It's time for you to leave.

She walks to the window, opens it.

Eurymachus! Gather your lackeys! Stoke
your fires! Tomorrow the queen chooses a
husband. Have your celebration. Haul wine
from your ships, mine is all drunk. Like the
bridegroom.

She closes the window.

TELEMACHUS   Every word you speak, Mother. Every turn
of your eye, causes me shame. Announcing
the wedding is my job and you rob me of
it. The palace, the lands, what's left of my
fortune stays with me. The choice of groom
is mine as well, and I will have it.

PENELOPE   And how will you have all that? Did Athena
teach you how to win over a hundred men
who want you dead? How will you manage
this trick, little Prince? If you figure it out,
get to it first thing in the morning. But if a
night's rest teaches you freedom, you'll
wake knowing I just bought you another
day of life.

TELEMACHUS, red-faced, remains silent.
PENELOPE continues.

The day you were born, your great general
Menalaus arrived to take Odysseus to war.
Your father hitched up his plow. He put an
ox side by side with an ass, took a sack of
salt, and went out to the fields. Menalaus
found Odysseus driving an ox and an ass in
circles, plowing salt into his fields, and was
ready to give him up for mad and leave for
Troy without him.

TELEMACHUS   You slander my father to teach me
cowardice.

PENELOPE   Not cowardice. Discretion. Subtlety. Tactics–

A scream comes from off.

Eurycleia–

PENELOPE starts to follow the sound.

TELEMACHUS   My servant, Mother. Tend your weaving.
I will attend the business of my house.

*TELEMACHUS runs off. Pause.
PENELOPE takes a ring of keys from
a hiding place, follows.*

15. THE SLAP

*The courtyard. EURYMACHUS is enjoying
himself with the other suitors. ANTINOUS
enters; MELANTHO is nearby.*

EURYMACHUS   Antinous... your face is always so sour.
You're back early, the reason must be good?

ANTINOUS   Telemachus gave them the slip. His ship
flew by, they gave chase and couldn't catch
him. I would have seen him at the harbour,
but no sign, he must have come up the far
side of the island.

*PENELOPE's window swings open, she leans
out.*

PENELOPE   Eurymachus! Gather your lackeys! Stoke
your fires! Tomorrow the queen chooses a
husband. Have your celebration. Haul wine
from your ships, mine is all drunk. Like the
bridegroom.

*She closes the window. A great cheer goes up
from the suitors, all save EURYMACHUS
and ANTINOUS.*

EURYMACHUS   What turns here? I don't like this move.

ANTINOUS   We've won.

EURYMACHUS   The bait stinks, I won't touch it. Slap my
                    face, Antinous. Come on. Hard.

                    ANTINOUS slaps him.

                    In front of all these witnesses? Melantho!
                    Carry a message to the queen. Her guest has
                    insulted me. I declare war on her household
                    and I will have it searched.

                    MELANTHO exits to the palace.

                    (*to ANTINOUS*) Take all of them. Find
                    Telemachus.

                    *ANTINOUS begins to exit; EURYCLEIA's
                    scream rings out of the palace.*

                    Antinous? Start with the queen's quarters.

                    ANTINOUS leads the suitors into the palace.

16. THE SCAR

                    *The STRANGER and EURYCLEIA, before a
                    steaming tub.*

STRANGER   Well what the hell is she doing that's so
                    bloody important?

EURYCLEIA   She's waiting for you to take a bath so you
                    don't smell so bloody much.

STRANGER   Her majesty might know there are better
                    islands than this one. Get back in there and
                    tell her I won't wait.

EURYCLEIA   And the minute I start thinking I can tell
                    a queen what to do is the minute I'll start
                    taking orders from a beggar. Now get your
                    bloody filthy clothes off.

STRANGER	I like my bloody filthy clothes the way they are.
EURYCLEIA	I can tell you're damn fond of them and all the crawly little friends you're sharing them with.
STRANGER	This is the king's house?
EURYCLEIA	When the king is at home, yes it is.
STRANGER	And you are the king's servant?
EURYCLEIA	When the king is at home, yes I am.
STRANGER	And I am the king's guest and the king's guest will not be abused by the king's servant or the king will have something to say about it.
EURYCLEIA	When the king gets home he can say what he likes but the queen says get in the tub, you stink!
STRANGER	And if I walk out this door and swim off the island, what will the queen have to say to you?
PENELOPE	*(from a distance)* Eurymachus! Gather your lackeys! Stoke your fires! Tomorrow the queen chooses a husband. Have your celebration. Haul wine from your ships, mine is all drunk. Like the bridegroom.
	The STRANGER and EURYCLEIA both slump.
EURYCLEIA	She's done it. It's for the best. What can you do? What can you do?
STRANGER	I feel old, Eurycleia. Leathery old skin. Bag of bones.
EURYCLEIA	Here.

She undresses him.

Not so old. It isn't the skin and the bones and the teeth. It's the eyes. We see too much. Feel too much. Too much heart.

STRANGER   Who can know a woman's heart? It changes with the moon.

EURYCLEIA   Ahh. You've fallen in love with my queen like everyone does. I can almost see her husband in your eyes, he looked on her like that.

STRANGER   Did you love him, this king?

EURYCLEIA   I love him as a son. I raised him from a child, I nursed him, I washed him, I know him from touch, every inch...

She suddenly begins to scream. The STRANGER grabs her hand away from his leg.

The scar! The boar's tusk!

STRANGER   Mad old woman, shut up!

EURYCLEIA   The wild boar that gored your flesh to the bone!

STRANGER   Quiet! Shut your mouth!

He fumbles to cover himself and grab her.

EURYCLEIA   I washed it, I tended it, I ran fingers on it every day, I know you, you're home, Odysseus!

She tries to embrace him but he holds her by the wrist and throat.

STRANGER   Old woman, would you have me dead?

> *TELEMACHUS enters, sees the*
> *STRANGER with his hand on*
> *EURYCLEIA's throat.*

TELEMACHUS   Stranger, is this how you return hospitality?

STRANGER   Excuse me. Am I speaking to a Prince?

TELEMACHUS   Prince Telemachus. I would have your name as well.

STRANGER   *(beat)* My name...

> *The STRANGER hesitates, overwhelmed.*

EURYCLEIA   *(beat)* He is your father.

TELEMACHUS   You're deceived old woman. My father is not coming home.

EURYCLEIA   These hands know him. This skin, these teeth, this heart, these old eyes–

TELEMACHUS   A god plays with your senses, I know my father's description – not so tall, not so old, not so faced, not so nosed, not so alive...

EURYCLEIA   Don't stand there, tell him!

STRANGER   The shape, the face, the years – none of them are mine. No hard work for a god to bring a man up or down in the world.

TELEMACHUS   Then a god amuses himself by ripping open old scars.

STRANGER   The god is Athena herself. She aged me, she made me what you see. All a disguise so I could enter my own home in safety.

TELEMACHUS   These are easy lies, any one of us could make the same claim, this old woman could be Odysseus as easily as you.

STRANGER	The day I left Ithaca, you were six hours old. King Menalaus arrived with his black ships to haul me off to war. I couldn't bear to leave you. I pretended I was mad, sowed salt into my fields. Menalaus went off to sail without me.
	But his brother, Agamemnon, saw through my trick. He tore you from your mother's arms, took you out to the field, and laid you on the earth, crying, in front of the moving plow. I turned the blade. And Agamemnon's men dragged me off to Troy.
	(beat) No other Odysseus will come. He and I are the same. His bitter fortune is mine, his wanderings are mine, his son, left twenty years without father, that son is mine. Twenty years away, I'm back on my island.
	TELEMACHUS melts, throws his arms around the STRANGER.
TELEMACHUS	I don't have to be king.
STRANGER	What? ...of course you'll be king.
TELEMACHUS	You're the king, I don't have to be king.
STRANGER	Not yet, but in time–
TELEMACHUS	I'm a soldier, I'm ready. We'll kill them all, tell me how.
STRANGER	Telemachus, there's a time for all–
TELEMACHUS	How do we do it? How do we manage a hundred?
EURYCLEIA	Tell the queen. I'll get her–
STRANGER	Stay there!
EURYCLEIA	No more waiting, you tell her now–

STRANGER	She will know, in her time!
EURYCLEIA	Twenty years! That's time!
STRANGER	Twenty years for her, yes, and twenty for me.
TELEMACHUS	We need a plan – there's a hundred of them, all armed–
STRANGER	We will have a plan–
EURYCLEIA	Do you have any idea what's been going on here?
STRANGER	No, and I will find out–
EURYCLEIA	She's been dying, dying of love for you–
STRANGER	I will not hear it from you!
TELEMACHUS	It's not true! She abuses your home–
EURYCLEIA	She is a paragon! She's protected both of you, every move she's made–
TELEMACHUS	She's behaved like a harlot, she's squandered your fortune–
STRANGER	Not a word! I will know my own wife! Penelope will know my truth, and I will know hers.
EURYCLEIA	You stubborn, imbecilic, mule-headed brat.
STRANGER	If the king has no queen there is no kingdom. Not a word from either of you. Leave us alone together – that's the only plan, until I know what I've come back to.

> *PENELOPE enters. Sounds of yelling, then pounding from a distance within the palace.*

PENELOPE	The suitors are in the hallways. They're searching the house. Looking for the crown prince, no doubt, with knives.
TELEMACHUS	Then I will go out to meet them.
STRANGER	*(pulling him back)* Your Highness... ill advised, if I may say.

> *TELEMACHUS sits back down. PENELOPE watches in amazement.*

PENELOPE	Seems I need to speak to my son with a deeper voice.

> *A pounding begins on the door, then a heavy thumping.*

	My husband was a master builder; they won't get in. We're here for the night. Telemachus, it's time you knew your father.
TELEMACHUS	My father?
PENELOPE	This boy needs instruction. Take up where you left off, my son will hear it.
STRANGER	I'm hardly the one to tell him...
PENELOPE	This family has been without husband and father for twenty years. My son needs his father's story. Take up where you left it.
STRANGER	The story is complicated...
PENELOPE	It draws closer to the heart, you said. Take it up.
STRANGER	To jump in at the middle we lose the thrust.
PENELOPE	Your audience waits, deliver the tale.

> *STRANGER looks to TELEMACHUS, who stares back in rapt attention. Beat.*

STRANGER	Odysseus fell in love. With a goddess.
PENELOPE	*(beat)* Well. The story *is* complicated.
TELEMACHUS	A *goddess*?
STRANGER	A goddess, yes. A witch.
PENELOPE	Poor Telemachus. Both your parents untrustworthy sluts.
STRANGER	Well, mother, a goddess. What choice did he have?
PENELOPE	What next? Did he escape with his pants barely on? She grew bored and kicked him out? Or did his men drag him away, kicking and screaming?
STRANGER	As I heard him tell it?
PENELOPE	Of course.
STRANGER	A goddess, you understand, is a being beyond our conception. Woman in form, and yet much more so. Woman in heart, and yet that heart is immortal, capable of feelings, understanding, subtleties... of love, that would conquer any mortal–
PENELOPE	The night may be long but my patience is not.
STRANGER	With no choice then but to venture into the house of a witch, Odysseus went to save his crew, where the gods had laid their trap for him.

Blackout.

17. THE SUITORS' SONG

*Unable to find TELEMACHUS, the suitors
console themselves with a drunken bawdy
ditty, to some sort of tune along the lines of a
Pogues-type rowdy English rugby song. The
lines might be divided up among the different
suitors, all repeat the last line of each verse.
Feel free to add pantomime.*

SUITORS

Ah sing me now all bards divine
The song that sweet enchants like wine
Sing of she that makes all lovers shine
The Golden Aphrodite.

All repeat the last line: The Golden Aphrodite

Now Aphrodite must be wed
Zeus chose his daughter's wedding bed
The god for the goddess of love he said
Is the blacksmith god Hephaistos.

*All repeat: The blacksmith god Hephaistos.
Etc.*

Hephaistos is an ugly Jack
With crippled legs and twisted back
He carried the goddess to his wedding shack
And she earned her wedding fee.

Well it wasn't long till seasons turned
Hephaistos love was not returned
But Aphrodite's passions burned
For the god of war named Ares.
(*all*) The studly god named Ares!

The goddess of love and the god of war
Made love in the ocean made love on the
   shore
Made love a thousand times or more
Immortals will not be denied.

Well Hephaistos he ranted, Hephaistos he
    choked
He hammered a chain that could never be
    broke
Finer than silk but stronger than oak
He set a fine trap for the lovers.

He draped silky chains from the top of his
    bed
An invisible web of invisible thread
Then went to his wife with his suitcase and
    said
"Honey I'm off on vacation."

Two seconds later a knock on the door
The wife is in bed with the great god of war
Then a shower of chains, and they don't
    move no more
They're in a tight situation.

"Well all you gods, look", Lord Hephaistos
    cries
"I've caught me a pair of adulterous flies
The love of my life now I only despise
The Golden Aphrodite."

Sly Hermes looks down on that golden pair
Nudges Apollo, says "I wouldn't care
Wrap me in chains and let all the gods stare
If I can lay with the Golden Aphrodite."

They applaud themselves and exit.

18. HERMES

*ODYSSEUS begins his climb up a cliff;
we hear pig sounds in the distance. As
ODYSSEUS travels up, HERMES —
messenger of the gods — comes down. The
scene takes place in mid-air.*

HERMES   Hail wanderer.

YOUNGER ODYSSEUS	Your downy lip marks you for a boy, but your manner says you are a god.
HERMES	Lonely man. I am Hermes, the gods' messenger. We watch your trek and are delighted by it, every turn a new surprise.
YOUNGER ODYSSEUS	You gods take entertainment as boys torture frogs.
HERMES	We don't force your torture, you trot so cheerfully to it yourself. Though Poseidon would have you dead for your treatment of his son, we others hold back his hand, such is our love for you.
YOUNGER ODYSSEUS	I would you showed me better love.
HERMES	Here then, a sign of it. We will not let you walk un-warned into the witch's warren. Why let our fun end there? Your friends turned to swine by Circe [SIR-see].
YOUNGER ODYSSEUS	To swine? Then I go warned.
HERMES	If you go to free them, you go to stay.
YOUNGER ODYSSEUS	Yet go I must.
HERMES	Marvelous. You are a wonder.

HERMES reveals a flower.

This plant I plucked for your protection.
So pure and potent is the flower
it will defeat the witch's spells.
She'll feed you drink to charm your eyes,
but this herb will keep your senses strong.

Then sweetness turns, she'll take her wand
to herd you squealing to her sty.
Take then out your cutting blade
and shine death's face back in her eyes.
She'll kneel and offer up her bed,
a god's delight you may not refuse.
But make her swear an oath to heaven,
She'll play no witch's trick upon you.
Before you trust immortal love
Her wand and scissors must be shed,
Else when time comes to leave those sheets
You'll leave your manhood in her bed.

YOUNGER
ODYSSEUS   ...Aye...?

HERMES   Oh, aye!

YOUNGER
ODYSSEUS   Hermes, your love I'll return at first
                    opportunity; a hundred black bulls to you
                    and Zeus I'll burn in supplication.

HERMES   Always, Odysseus, your love for the gods is
                    well observed. But I wonder on your course
                    to the witch's hut.

YOUNGER
ODYSSEUS   Bless me further. Wonder aloud.

HERMES   Her oath forestalls underhanded tricks;
                    The herb is proof against her spells.
                    But what hope for a man in a witch's bed?
                    You can always turn back now. Farewell.

                    *HERMES ascends. ODYSSEUS continues
                    the climb.*

19. CIRCE

> *Pig sounds grow; ODYSSEUS reaches CIRCE [SIR-see] at her house in the sky – she sees him in mid-climb. As they speak, PENELOPE, EURYCLEIA, and TELEMACHUS watch them, and the STRANGER watches PENELOPE.*

CIRCE   Hanging man.

YOUNGER ODYSSEUS   Goddess.

CIRCE   Your friends used the door, would you come by the window? You'll be my parrot. Or my monkey.

YOUNGER ODYSSEUS   Your sheep, Mistress, your lamb, your lizard on a wall, your guest.

CIRCE   So many choices. Take drink, traveller, honeyed wine, rest, make this your home.

> *ODYSSEUS moves to her level and tastes.*

YOUNGER ODYSSEUS   Sweet nectar.

> *He drains it in a draught.*

CIRCE   *(raising her stick)* Now, swine, to the sty and snore with your friends!

> *ODYSSEUS pulls his sword and takes it straight to her neck, crossing it with her wand.*

YOUNGER ODYSSEUS   But I'm wide awake, Goddess.

CIRCE   What kind of man are you?

YOUNGER ODYSSEUS	No swine, witch.
CIRCE	No mortal has ever drank this cup and stood on two legs.
YOUNGER ODYSSEUS	My name–
CIRCE	I know your name, Odysseus, Hermes has spoken it many times, foretelling the day you would come with your black ship. Put up your sword, this won't be our battlefield, friendship we'll have, not war between us. We shall mingle, make love we two. Mutual trust comes of play and love.
YOUNGER ODYSSEUS	Circe, do I look like a fawning boy? You'd have me sigh and take your hand?
CIRCE	No boy, warrior, I size you well.
YOUNGER ODYSSEUS	In this house you turn my men to swine. I'd be mad to follow to your dangerous bed.
CIRCE	Mad in the same part to refuse a goddess.
YOUNGER ODYSSEUS	You'd take my manhood while you have me stripped.
CIRCE	One part danger, three parts pleasure.
YOUNGER ODYSSEUS	No bed will I mount with you upon it.
CIRCE	Then kill or be killed. Will your knife cut a goddess?
YOUNGER ODYSSEUS	I'll have my crew.

CIRCE	Take them. Pork and ham to last your whole voyage.
YOUNGER ODYSSEUS	No other path for us?
CIRCE	Only one, have you the legs?
YOUNGER ODYSSEUS	Then swear me an oath, you'll vow my safety.
CIRCE	Strong Odysseus. What woman's bed did you last brave? A captured slave girl's? A Trojan whore's?
YOUNGER ODYSSEUS	No magic – swear it.
CIRCE	Mortal, you take liberties where you should fear for your life. I swear thee now, by Apollo above, by Hades below, by the gods and goddesses assembled at Olympus, I'll do no harm to Odysseus, in my bed or out of it, my goal is friendship, I seek love and trust.

> *The sword still between them, ODYSSEUS and CIRCE lean toward a kiss; PENELOPE watches them, the STRANGER watches PENELOPE.*

20. THE WEB

STRANGER	Well. With eyes open or shut, Odysseus overstepped his bounds and suffered terrible, exquisite love for it. Immortal, devastating, soul-rending–
PENELOPE	Tedious adjectives. Dig out the nub.
STRANGER	The nub is, at a year's end, of his own free will... Odysseus cleaved his heart in two to quit this sacred love... why?

TELEMACHUS	For his home. For his family.
PENELOPE	Damned propagandist. Who witnessed Penelope all these years? Who speaks for her?

Son and servant both remain silent.

Know this then. My son, full twenty years without his father. These last three years he's lived among these bandits in the hall, he's watched, seen my delays, flirtations, dalliance.... No surprise he's grown to hate his mother...

STRANGER	But you're not guilty...
PENELOPE	Of what?
STRANGER	Of this... dalliance?
PENELOPE	I'm not?

(to EURYCLEIA and TELEMACHUS) How did Penelope come to have one hundred and seven suitors? My craft – didn't you both witness it?

All of Ithaca demanded a new king. What power did I have to refuse? What woman is ever given power? The first suitors arrived.

"Just these?" I said. "I can't choose from these. Bring more."

More suitors came, and demanded my choice.

"With just these to choose, I'm to replace the great Odysseus?" I said. "More suitors, these won't suffice."

More came. I delayed, I made promises, I lied. Until outraged, they'd be put off no more.

"Wait," I said. "My father-in-law is near
death, and he has no proper burial shroud.
My shame will be great if I put marriage
before a daughter's obligations." And
I began to weave.

A great shroud. A web of such proportion it
might never be finished. And to be sure my
wedding day would not arrive too soon, all
the weaving I completed each day, at night
I unravelled. My endless web waxed and
waned with the moon. While the suitors
settled in for a siege, more arriving every
week, to eat and drink me out of my palace.

And why, son, why this great deceit? Why
Penelope's great craft?

> *TELEMACHUS stares at her in stony
> silence.*

STRANGER   Out of a great and faithful love such as the
world has never known. Such excellence of
craft, of wit, of fidelity...

PENELOPE   You own my son's heart. Instruct him.

STRANGER   You conquered a kingdom with skill to make
Medea herself jealous. The dogs came to
your door, you called more in to keep them
in check.

PENELOPE   *(pause)* Telemachus?

> *Pause.*

STRANGER   Your ingenious web... was meant to catch
time... until your husband's return.

> *Beat. Still no answer from TELEMACHUS,
> she turns the story.*

PENELOPE   My ingenious web was meant to catch so
many suitors they would bury the memory

of my famous sister, Helen. And I'm greatly
disappointed my game ends with the first
one hundred.

STRANGER   Her majesty is a liar.

PENELOPE   Your tongue forgets its audience.

STRANGER   If your game is over, open the door and let
in the contestants.

PENELOPE   If you think my game is over, you don't
know my husband's wife.

Pause. The STRANGER lets slip a smile.

STRANGER   My queen...

21. HADES

*YOUNGER ODYSSEUS untangles himself
from CIRCE.*

**YOUNGER
ODYSSEUS**   Home, Circe.

CIRCE   Strange man! You would leave a goddess
and wrestle with fate?

**YOUNGER
ODYSSEUS**   *Home*, Circe.

CIRCE   My great mortal friend, a part of me leaves
with you. How will you manage this great
voyage? Alone?

All you gods, beware! Odysseus will have
his way!

**YOUNGER
ODYSSEUS**   What other course is there for me?

CIRCE   Take instruction. For you, the only way
                       home is a hard way round, down first to the
                       House of Death.

YOUNGER
ODYSSEUS   The House of Death? It can't be done – the
                       only man to have returned is Heracles
                       himself – half a god!

CIRCE   You must risk the awesome one,
                       Persephone, Queen of the Dead. Seek there
                       the ghost of Tiresias [teye-REE-si-as], the
                       seer of Thebes, the great prophet. Only
                       Tiresias can chart your way home. Skirt past
                       Persephone, find the seer, and be gone
                       before the Queen of the Dead knows
                       you've been there.

                       As CIRCE describes the way, ODYSSEUS
                       hoists sails and rides the wind. The crew's
                       presence is muted for now, faded in the
                       background or even absent.

                       Odysseus, born for exploits, step your mast
                       and spread wide your canvas – catch the
                       North Wind to carry you across the River of
                       Ocean to Persephone's desolate shore. Run
                       the rip-tide, beach your ship, and find the
                       crumbling homes of Death. Cross Acheron
                       [A-ker-on] —the Flood of Grief—find the
                       place the River of Fire meets the River of
                       Tears, flowing out of Styx [sticks], the
                       Stream of Hate. There where the two rivers
                       thunder looms a stark crag.

                       Kneeling on the ground, ODYSSEUS
                       digs with his knife, following CIRCE's
                       instructions to perform the ritual.

                       Dig there a trench a forearm square and
                       around it pour libations out to all the dead –
                       first with honey mixed with milk, then with
                       sweet wine, third and last with water.
                       Sprinkle white barley and pray again and

again to all the faint dead, to all the helpless spirits of their ghosts...

YOUNGER ODYSSEUS

(kneeling before the trench, overlapping CIRCE) To all the spirits of your ghosts, I vow, once home in Ithaca I will slaughter my finest heifer, and burn for you the most tender parts in sacrifice. And to Lord Tiresias, I will offer a sleek black lamb, the finest of all my herds, thus to appease the nations of the dead.

These prayers I offer the nations of the dead in your dim glory, with this the blood of a black ewe and ram.

He pours blood from a bowl into the trench. Ghosts rise up around – they are pathetic, gliding spirits. ODYSSEUS pulls a sword to keep them from the blood.

TYRO

(approaching) Odysseus, I am Tyro [TEYE-roh], born of kings. Wife of Cretheus. Let me drink.

Before he can answer, more ghosts approach.

ANTIOPE

Odysseus, I am Asopus' [a-SOH-pus] daughter, Antiope [an-TEYE-oh-pee]. I slept with Zeus himself and bore him twin sons of greatness, let me drink.

MEGARA

I am Megara [ME-gar-a], magnanimous Creon's daughter, wed to the stalwart Heracles [HER-a-kleez], let me drink.

MINOS

Odysseus, I am Minos [MEYE-nos], illustrious son of Zeus. Let me drink.

ORION

Odysseus, I am Orion, the hunter, let me drink.

ALCMENA

I am Alcmena [alk-MEE-na], mother of Heracles. Let me drink.

JOCASTA   I am Jocasta, mother of Oedipus, wife of
                Oedipus, mother of pain, wife of pain. Let
                me drink.

ANTICLEIA   Odysseus? You're not dead...

**YOUNGER
ODYSSEUS**   Mother... you here?

                *ODYSSEUS lifts his sword, ANTICLEIA
                drinks.*

                What brought you down here, Mother?

                *As he speaks, he reaches to touch her, but her
                hand, her body, her clothes always float out of
                reach.*

ANTICLEIA   No wasting illness. No swift death. Only my
                loneliness for you. These years of pining.
                With no end.

**YOUNGER
ODYSSEUS**   Mother–

                He reaches again, she floats away again.

                –tell me of my father, tell me of my son, tell
                me of Penelope.

ANTICLEIA   She waits. They all wait.

**YOUNGER
ODYSSEUS**   Mother, let me hold you one last time...

ANTICLEIA   This place isn't for you. Our muscles, our
                bones, our sinews, everything burnt on our
                funeral pyres. These mists are all that are
                left.

                The sound of a bell in the distance.

                The Queen of the Dead draws near. No more
                time, fly back to the sun before she comes.

*ANTICLEIA steps back. ODYSSEUS sees
AJAX, sulking at a distance, calls out
desperately.*

**YOUNGER
ODYSSEUS** Ajax, great warrior, come drink the blood
of life! We quarreled in life – now even in
death, you won't forgive me? I'll give you
news of the war – conquer your rage, set
aside your pride.

*AJAX turns away, the bell sounds again,
slightly closer. ODYSSEUS spots another
figure approaching.*

Great Achilles!

*ODYSSEUS offers ACHILLES drink,
speaking more urgently now. As they speak,
the bell ringing sounds still closer.*

We honoured you as a god when you lived,
and now here you are, a mighty king over
the dead.

ACHILLES Don't waste pretty words about death on
me, Odysseus. Glory is for the living. For the
dead, there's nothing. Tell me only this. My
son – what news of my son?

**YOUNGER
ODYSSEUS** First in all battles, first in debate; in the belly
of the great wooden horse, he alone never
shook with fear, he alone emerged the
sacking of Troy without a scar...

ACHILLES *(turning away, swelling with pride)* My son...
my son...

IPHIGENIA Odysseus, I am Iphigenia [if-i-je-NEYE-a].
Let me drink.

CLYTEMNESTRA Odysseus, I am Clytemnestra [kleye-tem-
NES-tra]. Let me drink.

AGAMEMNON   Odysseus, you know me.

**YOUNGER
ODYSSEUS**   Agamemnon – old friend... death so soon?

AGAMEMNON drinks.

AGAMEMNON   My wife, Odysseus. My own accursed wife, Clytemnestra, and her lover. I returned from Troy, she sat me to feast, then cut me down with a club like some ox at a trough. Butchered in my own palace.

**YOUNGER
ODYSSEUS**   Clytemnestra – that name will be damned for all time.

AGAMEMNON   All of them. Even your own wife – when you reach home land your ship in secret, let her have no warning, leave nothing in the open. The time for trusting women is gone forever.

The bell rings, much closer now.

**YOUNGER
ODYSSEUS**   Agamemnon, stay, speak longer. Of Troy, of our youth, I want to share words with you.

AGAMEMNON   Troy is a dead man's memory. If Persephone comes upon you, you'll stay here with this joyless bunch. No glory among the dead, Odysseus.

AGAMEMNON moves away. The blind seer TIRESIAS approaches.

TIRESIAS   Odysseus, master of tactics, unluckiest man alive. Why leave the warm sun to visit the cold dead in this joyless place?

**YOUNGER
ODYSSEUS**   Tireseias – Seer of Thebes.

TIRESEIAS drinks the blood.

TIRESIAS You seek some easy way home, great captain. But only anguish lies ahead.

YOUNGER ODYSSEUS Is there yet a path for me?

TIRESIAS You will never escape the earth-shaker Poseidon. He follows your journey, bent on avenging the eye you tore from his son's head. Only one hope remains for a swift journey home.

Bell.

You will reach the island of the sun god, where his cattle graze, fat and numberless. Hunger will strike you but leave the beasts unharmed, nothing escapes the god of the sun. Deny yourself, restrain your crew and you may soon see your island. Raid those cattle, and I see your ship and company, all destroyed.

Bell.

Even if you alone escape, you'll have years ahead before you reach home, a broken man, and find a world of pain there – crude, arrogant men devour your fortune, court your wife, conspire to steal your very home.

Bell.

Aye, those men who haunt your palace will indeed pay in blood.

Bell.

But no peace for Odysseus until you win Poseidon's forgiveness. You must take up an oar and walk the earth, away from the sea, until you reach a place where men have never heard of the oceans or great Poseidon himself. Build a great mound there to the god of the seas, and plant your oar atop. Only then will you live a long life, ending in a death as gentle as this hand of mist.

The bell is nearly upon us now.

YOUNGER ODYSSEUS

All my companions? Every one of them dead? If I'm punished with years, what of my wife? My son, my home?

TIRESIAS

All these around you are dead, Odysseus. What if Persephone comes upon you here, carrying some snake-filled gorgon's head to shine upon you?

Other ghosts appear, crowding in on ODYSSEUS.

IPHIMEDEIA

Odysseus, I am Iphimedeia [eye-fi-me-DEYE-a], mother of giants, let me drink...

SISYPHUS

Odysseus, I am Sisyphus [SIS-i-fus], some say I am your father, let me drink...

TITYUS

I am Tityus [TI-ti-yus], vultures eat my liver, let me drink...

TANTALUS

I am Tantalus [TAN-ta-lus], tortured with thirst, let me drink...

PHAEDRA

I am Phaedra [FEE-dra]...

ARIADNE

I am Ariadne [a-ri-AD-nee]...

LEDA

I am Leda [LEE-da]...

The ghosts' cries grow to a crescendo, then cut dead; only PENELOPE, TELEMACHUS, EURYCLEIA, and the STRANGER are left visible.

PENELOPE   Glory is for the living. The glorious living. Where heroes sneak home in disguise on advice from an old friend. Where heroes clear the villains out of their homes, only to slink off again in the night, a great oar on the shoulder. Twenty years. My god, twenty years.

STRANGER   *(beat)* My queen...

PENELOPE stops him.

Penelope...

PENELOPE   All I want from you, Stranger, is the story.

STRANGER   *(beat)* What Zeus sends us... can we choose anything else but to bear it?

No answer. Beat.

Into the home of Death and out alive? Most men visit that place only once, you're doomed to see it twice. Arm your mind, there's worse ahead.

22. THE SIRENS

The song of the Sirens begins, very softly, a whisper at a distance. The crew boards the ship and begins rowing.

SIRENS   Famous man, hear our song, moor your ship, moor your ship.
No sail passes, without hearing, honeyed songs, from our lips.
We sing of Troy, we know of Troy, ten years of Troy, all of Troy.
Turn back time, end the voyage, all stops here, all stops here.

CIRCE appears, an apparition on the waves to guide ODYSSEUS.

CIRCE

The island of the Sirens, those creatures who enchant any man that approaches. Anyone who catches the Sirens' crying beauty will never see his lady, never return to his children's beaming faces. The Sirens will bewitch his mind from him, lure him to the rocks where they sit on corpses piled in the sun, ragged skin hanging on bones....
There's no avoiding the place, only preparation...

The crew all pack beeswax in their ears. Some of them lash ODYSSEUS to the mast.

YOUNGER ODYSSEUS

Take the beeswax, stop your ears up, pack it firm. Tie me fast, if I beg to be released, add more rope and lash it tighter...

The ship passes before the SIRENS as they sing to ODYSSEUS.

SIRENS

Famous man, hear our song, moor your
    ship, moor your ship.
No sail passes, without hearing, honeyed
    songs, from our lips.
We sing of Troy, we know of Troy, ten years
    of Troy, all of Troy.
Turn back time, end the voyage, all ends
    here, all ends here.

We know your wounds, we know your
    pains,
We know your journey, we know your trials.
Weary sailors, here take joy, leave this place,
    wiser men.
We sing of Troy, we know of Troy, ten years
    of Troy, all of Troy.
All ends here, sweet death. All ends here,
    sweet death.

The song fades, the men untie ODYSSEUS; he collapses in sobs.

23. SCYLLA AND CHARYBDIS

CIRCE again appears as breakers begin to beat loudly.

CIRCE   Up, up. No time to recover.

No choice now, Odysseus. Your course lies a narrow channel guarded by two dreaded monsters.

Atop a crag of rock, hidden in the clouds, lurks Scylla, the six-headed devastation. Scylla's six mouths gape with three rows of razor teeth; her six serpent necks hang down through the mist to feed on whatever quarry comes beneath; not a ship has ever passed without losing one man to every one of her six gullets.

Across the strait stands a second crag, not an arrow shot away. Beneath it lies Charybdis, monster of the deep. Three times a day she gulps the ocean down and three times a day spits it back up. Come upon her whirlpool or her waterspout, not even the earthquake god could save you.

YOUNGER ODYSSEUS   Two monsters guarding the same strait – how do I fight both at once?

CIRCE   Man of war, will glorious battle never leave your heart? Yield to fate, Odysseus, there is no fighting these monsters, they are an immortal nightmare. Your course is to perch at the spout's edge, wait the moment of calm water, and shoot the channel at a racing stroke. Pay Scylla her toll of lives and never let your eye stray from Charybdis – better by far to grieve six men than to lose your entire ship and crew.

**YOUNGER
ODYSSEUS**   Circe – the task is impossible. How can
I prepare my crew for it?

CIRCE   You can't.

   ODYSSEUS turns to address the crew.

**YOUNGER
ODYSSEUS**   Friends, we've met danger before. I gave us
victory at Troy, I won our freedom at the
Cyclops' cave – this is no worse. All eyes to
your oars, all work as one and we'll outlast
this terror!

STRANGER   He handed out orders, readied the men to
face dangers in the water, but about the
danger from above, he said nothing, as they
could do nothing. And clearing his mind of
all Circe had said, Odysseus prepared for
the fight.

   *ODYSSEUS pulls on armour, takes up a
   sword at the helm as the crew rows towards
   the crags.*

CIRCE   Hell-bent again, Odysseus?

**CIRCE &
STRANGER**   It's time to bow to the deathless gods
themselves.

   *Ignoring the advice, in full armour,
   ODYSSEUS stands at the bow, his eyes
   always upwards looking for SCYLLA.*

CREW   Cauldron ahead! Turn!

**YOUNGER
ODYSSEUS**   She's spitting! Hold fast!

CREW MEMBER   Water spout! Three hundred feet high!

**YOUNGER
ODYSSEUS**   Stand in her spray! Wait till she drops!

CREW MEMBER   Turn back!

Helmsman, steer clear!

**YOUNGER
ODYSSEUS**   Steady Helmsman! Hold water! Mark this point until I command!

CREW MEMBER   No way through, turn or she'll yaw!

**YOUNGER
ODYSSEUS**   Hold! Steady oars! Ready! At the ready!

CREW MEMBER   She's calm! The spout's down!

**YOUNGER
ODYSSEUS**   Pull now! Pull! Pull! Pull!

From behind him, voices call.

CREW MEMBERS   Odysseus!

Odysseus!

Odysseus!

Odysseus!

Odysseus!

Odysseus!

ODYSSEUS turns to stern, waving a sword at an unseen menace.

STRANGER   All eyes fixed on Charybdis, Scylla snatched six men from the ship, hooking them like little fish, wriggling, gasping for their lives.

YOUNGER ODYSSEUS   Where is she? Hell's bitch! I've seen your home, you won't take any more!

CREW MEMBER   Whirlpool! Turn back!

Hade's mouth! Pull it about!

YOUNGER ODYSSEUS   *(turning back to the bow)* Ahead! All pull! Fast through! Hard the way!

CREW MEMBER   Captain, we're turning!

YOUNGER ODYSSEUS   On your oars! Strike the swells! Churn the water! Trust in Zeus to pull us through alive!

CREW MEMBER   Oarsmen pull!

Helmsman, steer by the crags or you plunge us all to ruin!

YOUNGER ODYSSEUS   All speed! Pull as one!

CREW MEMBERS   Past the crag! Make the crag!

She won't get us! We're through, pull boys!

More screams as more men are snatched.

Odysseus!

Odysseus!

Odysseus!

YOUNGER ODYSSEUS   They're gone! Tears later! Pull before she strikes again!

ALL CREW   Pull! Pull! Pull!

Pull! Pull! Pull!

Softer.

Pull! Pull! Pull!

Pull! Pull! Pull!

24. THE CATTLE OF THE SUN

Only a tiny fraction of the original crew remains, exhausted, having cleared the whirlpool. They hug each other in exhaustion and mourning.

JONESY Land!

EURYLOCHUS An island.... Pull oars, we make dry land tonight!

YOUNGER ODYSSEUS Hold. Not here.

EURYLOCHUS Are you flesh and blood, Odysseus?

YOUNGER ODYSSEUS That's the Island of the Sun. Tieresias warned us of this place. We won't land here.

EURYLOCHUS What are you made of?

JONESY Captain–

EURYLOCHUS Every turn you take us our numbers are cut in half. Night is on us, we're falling asleep at the oars and you say no landing? Night demands we get ashore before some god is tempted to sink us once and for all in a black storm!

JONESY We're cursed, Captain, not you. Give us one chance to catch a meal on dry land.

EURYLOCHUS We'll eat on land tonight and pull out at dawn. Aye?

ALL CREW Aye!

**YOUNGER
ODYSSEUS** Men, this is fate playing with you. Swear me this. No cattle, no sheep on this island will be harmed. Circe provided food and wine, only that we will eat and drink.

ALL CREW Sworn.

STRANGER But as soon as they landed, fate played her hand. Zeus blew up a storm, holding them to the island. Gales blew, day in, day out, a full month without rest. The men held to their pledge so long as Circe's supplies held. But when the last of the barley was eaten, when their angling hooks dangled empty, thin bellies demanded a new alliance.

The men lie baking on the sand, exhausted, famished in the sun. With ODYSSEUS absent, EURYLOCHUS speaks to the remaining crew.

EURYLOCHUS We've seen every form of torment ever handed out by the sea and the gods. But famine is the worst of all. Let's pick out the fattest cattle and offer up a sacrifice to the god of the sun. Then we feed ourselves. If we can't choose when we'll die, at least let's take a hand in how. Not by starvation – I'll die on the sea quick and watery! Like an ordinary man.

*They set at preparing their meal.
ODYSSEUS comes upon them.*

STRANGER When Odysseus returned, the smell of flesh roasted in the air. Zeus had conspired against them, the cattle of the sun god lay slaughtered.

> *Odysseus clutches them, weeps for them.*

The sky cleared. They stepped the mast, set sail, and Zeus piled a thunderhead above the ship. The squall struck with gale force. The mast toppled. The boat split. Every crewman went down.

Odysseus alone clung to a timber, as the waves carried him once again, to an island. Where he lay captive, seven years at the whim of the gods, kept alive only by the sight in his mind's eye, of home and family.

> *The YOUNGER ODYSSEUS drifts into the distance, hanging on to his mast, until out of sight.*

> *Pause. Slowly, PENELOPE applauds.*

PENELOPE   Bravo.

TELEMACHUS   Good god, Mother! A stone would shed more tears for my father!

PENELOPE   Tears? At what? It's a marvellous story! Witches! Giants! Six-headed monsters! Wonderful tale, I'm sure you'll dine on it for years to come.

EURYCLEIA   My queen, show your heart, this once...

STRANGER   Show your love, Queen. Odysseus waits on it.

PENELOPE   You woo for him, speak love for him, will you kill his enemies and make love to his wife as well?

STRANGER   Not this broken down old man. Just show one sign of your love. Odysseus will return as you remember him, young and strong.

PENELOPE   And what sign do I have of his?

STRANGER   One man to battle one hundred. I'd say
                that's some offer.

PENELOPE   I have a hundred offers downstairs. I'll have
                dearer stuff put up against my kingdom.

STRANGER   The dearer stuff is your husband's life...

PENELOPE   I wait, and my son grows up without a
                father. I wait, and Ithaca demands a new
                king. I wait, and my son disappears in the
                night–

STRANGER   If you're looking for blame, put it on the
                gods–

PENELOPE   I wait and my husband sneaks home in
                disguise–

STRANGER   Your husband comes home and risks a
                thousand deaths to do it–

PENELOPE   I wait and my husband leaves me again to
                take up the great adventure. Give me an
                ordinary man, I want no more heroes.

STRANGER   Your husband is home. He will have his wife
                and his kingdom.

PENELOPE   There is no king until the queen names him.

STRANGER   And your time ticks, Madame – you set the
                clock yourself...

                She goes to the window.

PENELOPE   Wake up, my suitors! The wedding contest
                begins now!

                She exits. EURYCLEIA follows her out.

STRANGER   Bluff! All contrary, obstinate bluff!

TELEMACHUS   I don't think she's bluffing–

STRANGER	That is the most damnable female that has ever lived and I have run into every form of them in earth, heaven and hell!
TELEMACHUS	Father, we fight now, yes?
STRANGER	That's not the woman I married. I married a girl of intelligence and wit, of charm, of sense.
TELEMACHUS	We need a plan.
STRANGER	A man falls in love with a girl of twenty, but they're born with all the skins of a snake.
TELEMACHUS	There are a hundred of them–
STRANGER	She was a blossom when I met her, you understand? Not this ripe musty old fruit. She was gentle, kind.
TELEMACHUS	Mother?
STRANGER	Telemachus, I am trying to tell you something about women: Beware!
TELEMACHUS	But we will fight them still?
STRANGER	Oh, we fight. But how, that's the question.
TELEMACHUS:	You don't have a plan?
STRANGER	Two against a hundred. That's not something to look forward to.
TELEMACHUS:	Father... you have a prophesy. You're going to win.
STRANGER	The gods are misers with prophesy. They never say how.
	Get my bow from the armoury and every weapon you can carry, we pick the strongest position available, strike at the best moment

that presents itself, and fight till your arm falls off.

TELEMACHUS   That's insanity.

STRANGER   If Athena protects you, you'll survive any-thing.

TELEMACHUS   What if Athena isn't protecting me?

STRANGER   Then you haven't a hope of seeing tomorrow no matter what.

TELEMACHUS   But how do I know if she's protecting me or she isn't?

STRANGER   You'll know because when it's over you'll be the one who walks away.

TELEMACHUS   But how–

STRANGER   No more asking, just do.

TELEMACHUS   But how do–

STRANGER   There isn't any other choice, that's how we do it.

TELEMACHUS   But how do you–

STRANGER   Because I'm your father and I love you.

STRANGER exits, TELEMACHUS follows.

25. THE CONTEST OF THE BOW

The Courtyard. The suitors are gathered, the STRANGER stands apart from them. TELEMACHUS slips in unseen by the suitors, approaches the STRANGER, slips a sword from his own coat to the STRANGER's.

TELEMACHUS	It's all I could get.
STRANGER	One sword?
TELEMACHUS	The armoury is bolted.
STRANGER	Then find the key.
TELEMACHUS	It's never been bolted my whole life, I don't know of any key.
STRANGER	She's locked the armoury. What does she expect me to do, kill them all with my teeth?
TELEMACHUS	She doesn't know it's you.
STRANGER	I think she's figured it out, don't you?
TELEMACHUS	She wouldn't lock the armoury if she knew it was you...
STRANGER	And just how well do you know your mother?
TELEMACHUS	How could she know? Just tell her, she'll give you the key...
STRANGER	Look – men and women – how you do things is important – there are times when you just know. We do not ask for the key!
TELEMACHUS	Why not?
STRANGER	Because that's how we do it. Where's your sword?
TELEMACHUS	*(shows STRANGER a knife from under his coat)* I've got this.

> *STRANGER pushes the sword back to TELEMACHUS, takes the knife. Meanwhile EURYCLEIA has entered with MELANTHO, approaching the suitors.*

EURYCLEIA	No weapons, you heard. The Queen's orders – out the door with them.
SUITOR	You aren't having my sword, granny.
EURYCLEIA	Then out the door with you. Bunch of drunks with swords – when the queen announces her choice, you'll be cutting into each other and the house full of blood. Weapons gone or you are, go on!

As she passes through them, the suitors grumble and turn their weapons over to MELANTHO. PENELOPE appears on a platform.

PENELOPE	Gentlemen. Three years you've invaded my house. Three years you've asked to take the place of my husband, the great and revered Odysseus. Some of you might remember him; you were children when he became king.
TELEMACHUS	*(aside to STRANGER)* I don't get it. Why don't we just ask for the key?
STRANGER	Shh! This is good...
PENELOPE	Perhaps if one of you princes could match him for wit, it would make my choice easier. Perhaps if one of you came close to him in intelligence, I'd find an easy match. If there were one among you with his breeding, one who shared his reverence for the gods, his love for the world, for beauty, his horror at cruelty... I loved my husband for these things. I've looked among you, I haven't found them.
STRANGER	You hear that? There's her sign. She loves me.
PENELOPE	But I can compromise. I've seen signs lately of his charm, his way with words, his talent

for lying. But that's not quite enough. If there were only one in this palace with the quality of righteousness I remember – there'd be something in that. If there were one with a sense of justice – that's a mark for a king. If one in this courtyard had his courage, his leadership, his tact.... His manners, his grace, his kindness, his sense of Honour.... I'm disappointed again.

TELEMACHUS   How do you know she loves you?

STRANGER   She despises me. She truly does. Forget the swords, it's over.

PENELOPE   But I can compromise. My husband was master of every craft, I'll measure just one. Here is my husband's hunting bow – it once belonged to Heracles. If any among you can string this bow, then pick your target. The best shot wins the bride. One hundred and seven arrows, one for each of you.

     She sets the bow and a quiver of arrows out for the suitors. A moment's silence.

STRANGER   *(aside to TELEMACHUS)* Goddamn, that's a hell of a woman.

DORION   *Heracle's* bow? What, the great Odysseus doesn't own a bow of Apollo's? Let me try that bow!

     DORION steps up, the suitors laugh and cheer. DORION tries to bend the bow for stringing. Tries again. Can't bend it an inch.

     (panting) Bloody... hell of a.... That's some bow.

     The suitors laugh.

EURYMACHUS   I'll give you a hand, Dorion. In fact, I'll use two.

DORION	You're the wedding broker, Eurymachus. You're not in the contest.
EURYMACHUS	I'm the best archer in all the islands. You don't expect me to pass up an archery contest?
DORION	You're a lying scum and I nearly trusted you.
	EURYMACHUS smiles, takes the bow. He bends it... perhaps an inch farther than Dorion. The suitors laugh.
EURYMACHUS	Boletus! Give us a hand here. You bend it, I'll string it.
BOLETUS	*(stepping up)* I'll bend it. I'll string it. I'll shoot it.
EURYMACHUS	If there's only one man here among us who can bend this bow, it's you, but I'm sure as hell the one to beat.
BOLETUS	Is it my turn or is it not?
	EURYMACHUS gives up the bow. All suitors hush. He bends it, but not nearly halfway. The suitors are quiet, dumbfounded.
	We're done. The bow defeats us.
STRANGER	*(pushing TELEMACHUS forward)* Now!
TELEMACHUS	*(startled)* I'll try it!
	The suitors laugh.
EURYMACHUS	Telemachus! We've been looking all over for you!
TELEMACHUS	And here I am in my own house. I'll try my father's bow, it's my right above all others.

EURYMACHUS	And what if you succeed? You'll marry your mother?
TELEMACHUS	I'll choose her husband as is my right and we'll all be happy.

> BOLETUS *holds the bow out to* TELEMACHUS *who comes forth to take it. More laughter and cheers.* TELEMACHUS *leans on the bow, bends it, and it bends, beautifully. About to loop the bowstring, grinning and amazed, he looks out to the* STRANGER. *The* STRANGER *signals him "no". A pause, then* TELEMACHUS *suddenly lets the bow spring back.*

	(*panting*) Damn. Once a weakling always a weakling.
STRANGER	I'll try it!
EURYMACHUS	You again?
ANTINOUS	Out old filth! Back to the street!
TELEMACHUS	Each man chooses the next, that's the pattern, I choose the Stranger.
EURYMACHUS	This is disgusting! You would allow an old tramp to enter a contest for your mother's hand?
PENELOPE	The contest is open. Let him try the bow.

> *The suitors laugh as the* STRANGER *takes the bow.*

DORION	Look at him! He's a lover of old bows!
BOLETUS	A connoisseur of old bows!
ASTEUS	Maybe it's just like the one he has at home!

> *Drawing a breath, the STRANGER leans on*
> *the bow; it resists. The suitors burst out*
> *laughing again. Panting and suddenly*
> *looking very old, he bends again and it gives*
> *an inch or two.*

AMPHINIMOUS   Come on old man!

ANTINOUS   Just like the good old days, Gramps! Heave!

> *A suitor steps forward to take the bow.*

EURYMACHUS   Give it up, old Rotbag.

PENELOPE   *(looking worried for the first time)* Stand back!

> *The suitor stops. Respectfully steps back.*
> *Pause. TELEMACHUS steps forward.*

TELEMACHUS   Father? I can help?

> *The STRANGER, still panting, waves him*
> *off.*

PENELOPE   We'll have a recess – grease the bow and warm it on the fire–

> *In one great effort, the STRANGER forces*
> *the bow down, bending it until strung. He*
> *notches an arrow. He is panting, hardly*
> *looking as if he's up to what's ahead.*

STRANGER   Telemachus. The guest you welcomed has not disgraced you. *(to suitors)* Yellow dogs. Plunder my house, attack my son, assault my wife. Contempt for the gods, contempt for men. Breathe your last, you die in blood.

> *A magical slaughter ensues. TELEMACHUS*
> *with sword guards his father; the*
> *STRANGER rains arrows until every suitor*
> *lies dead. When it's done, TELEMACHUS*
> *stands among the bodies; the STRANGER*
> *sinks down on a bench, unable to stand*
> *another moment.*

(*panting*) Sulfer and fire. Scour my hall with fumes. Purify this palace.

26. THE OLIVE TREE BED

Fires are lit. The STRANGER sits, still shaken, trying to recover. His hand wanders over his face, feeling the wrinkles, the unfamiliar features, struck by a miracle that hasn't happened. PENELOPE stands apart, staring in wonder at him.

STRANGER It's not my face, Penelope. It's not my form. But it's me.

TELEMACHUS Mother – It's Odysseus. Go to him.

Beat.

He's back now, you know it's him.

Beat.

EURYCLEIA For godssakes, look for yourself – he has the scar, it's him.

Beat.

STRANGER These aren't my years, either. Athena disguised me. She'll restore me.

Beat.

PENELOPE (*softly*) Will she?

TELEMACHUS Athena disguised him, she'll restore him, she's a god, she can do anything.

PENELOPE The gods give us years of hardship. We don't often get to give them back.

STRANGER Eurycleia... gather the women in this house who rutted with the suitors. Set them to

cleaning the blood... and then Telemachus,
in the morning we'll give them a swift death
by our swords. Now leave us, your mother
and I know one another better than anyone.
We have our own secret signs.

TELEMACHUS   I swear I'll give no clean death to those
trulls. I'll hang them from a hawser across
the palace top, toes dangling, like doves
caught in a snare. Their heels will dance
one last time, but not for long.

TELEMACHUS turns to go.

PENELOPE   Telemachus. If this stranger has one more
trick in him, you will be here to see it.

*He looks to his father for confirmation;
ODYSSEUS doesn't return the glance.*

STRANGER   We won't play this last round here.

*Tired, he pulls himself to his feet, approaches
her.*

Come Penelope–

PENELOPE   If my husband saw your hand on me, he'd
cut it off your corpse.

EURYCLEIA   Madame–!

TELEMACHUS   He *is* your husband!

PENELOPE   Have both of you gone soft? There are all
sorts of gods. Any of them can pull the trick
of appearing to be a man, any man at all.

EURYCLEIA   That's no god, it's an ordinary man–

PENELOPE   Ordinary? Then it cannot be my husband.
My husband will never be an ordinary man.

STRANGER By your own contest, I am your husband, with a marriage fee of one hundred men paid in advance.

PENELOPE For your services I thank you. I'll pay you well for it and send you on your way.

STRANGER *Pay* me? Out of my own treasures?

EURYCLEIA For heaven's sake, look at him!

PENELOPE You thick old woman. Anyone could walk in and announce he's master of the house and you'd fall at his knees. Just throw a rug on the floor for him and make sure he's gone in the morning.

STRANGER I *will* be gone. Make up a bed in the hall, nurse, I'll sleep alone tonight.

PENELOPE If he wants the king's bed, he can have it. Take the bed from our bridal chamber, nurse. Move it out to the hall and let the stranger sleep wherever he likes.

STRANGER Woman, what are you saying? *Our* bed? It *can't* be moved...

Beat. Caught and knowing it, ODYSSEUS goes on.

I built this house around that bed.

I carved the bedpost from an olive tree; that olive tree still rooted in the ground.

I planed it, drilled it, inlaid it with silver, gold and ivory. I carved three other posts to match, stretched a web between them, a hide of gleaming crimson.

Our bedroom I built around that bed, this house I built around that room, this house stands at the middle of our kingdom and our love.

There is our secret pact and pledge, no eyes
ever to see it but our own and this old
woman. The last trick is played, Penelope,
tell me at last. Does our pledge stand, or has
another cut the olive trunk and hauled our
bed away?

Pause.

PENELOPE   Could any ordinary man build such a bed,
Odysseus?

Our bed stands. After twenty years, it
stands.

Telemachus, your father gave you a task.

*TELEMACHUS slowly walks to his mother.
He goes to his knees, kisses her hand, then
exits; EURYCLEIA follows.*

STRANGER   My love. You've won the last trick.

PENELOPE   Never. Always one more round to be played.
Come. In the morning you take up your oar
and go do the gods' work. Let's take what's
left of this night.

STRANGER   I won't take that oar, Penelope.

PENELOPE   Escape fate, Odysseus? You of all men know
it can't be done.

STRANGER   The gods took our youth, Penelope. I can't
give them our old age as well.

PENELOPE   Not old, Odysseus. Not old at all.

STRANGER   Not old? Look at us. If I manage this last
trip, I come home to be buried.

PENELOPE   The two of us? We'll live forever. You with
your great horse. Me with my great web.
We're immortal, you and I.

STRANGER   My great love. If I hadn't made it home to
                   you, what a sad and ordinary life it would
                   have been.

PENELOPE   To bed now. And then our stories. I won't
                   close my eyes until we've shared every
                   word, yours and mine.

                       They exit. ATHENA enters to sing a sweet
                       coda.

ATHENA   Father Zeus give one last gift
                   Hold the dawn, keep back the light
                   Stretch out this new wedding night
                   Till these lovers know they're home

                   Youthful Dawn don't leave your bed
                   Rest your fingertips of rose
                   Keep morning close beneath your sheets
                   Till these lovers know their home

                   Let this old couple have their night
                   Touch the masks, take off the roles
                   Let them walk this one last island
                   Till these lovers know their home

                       The end.

Rick Chafe was born in Toronto, raised in Winnipeg. His other plays include *Zac and Speth*, *The Last Man and Woman on Earth*, and he co-authored *Parables and Paradoxes*, based on the shorter stories of Franz Kafka. He freelances as a documentary and educational videomaker and teacher.

OTHER TITLES
BY RICK CHAFE

The Book of Questions
In *Instant Applause*
1 act   1m/1f
ISBN: 921368380
$19.95

Zac and Speth
Two teenagers run away to Vancouver where they
learn about neo-anarchism, run afoul of the law,
and spend the next ten years trying to sort out
their love affair and stop the American
annexation of Canada.
1 act   1m/1f
ISBN: 1551739852
$7.00

Available from Playwrights Union of Canada
416-703-0201   fax 703-0059
orders@puc.ca   http://www.puc.ca